DISCARD

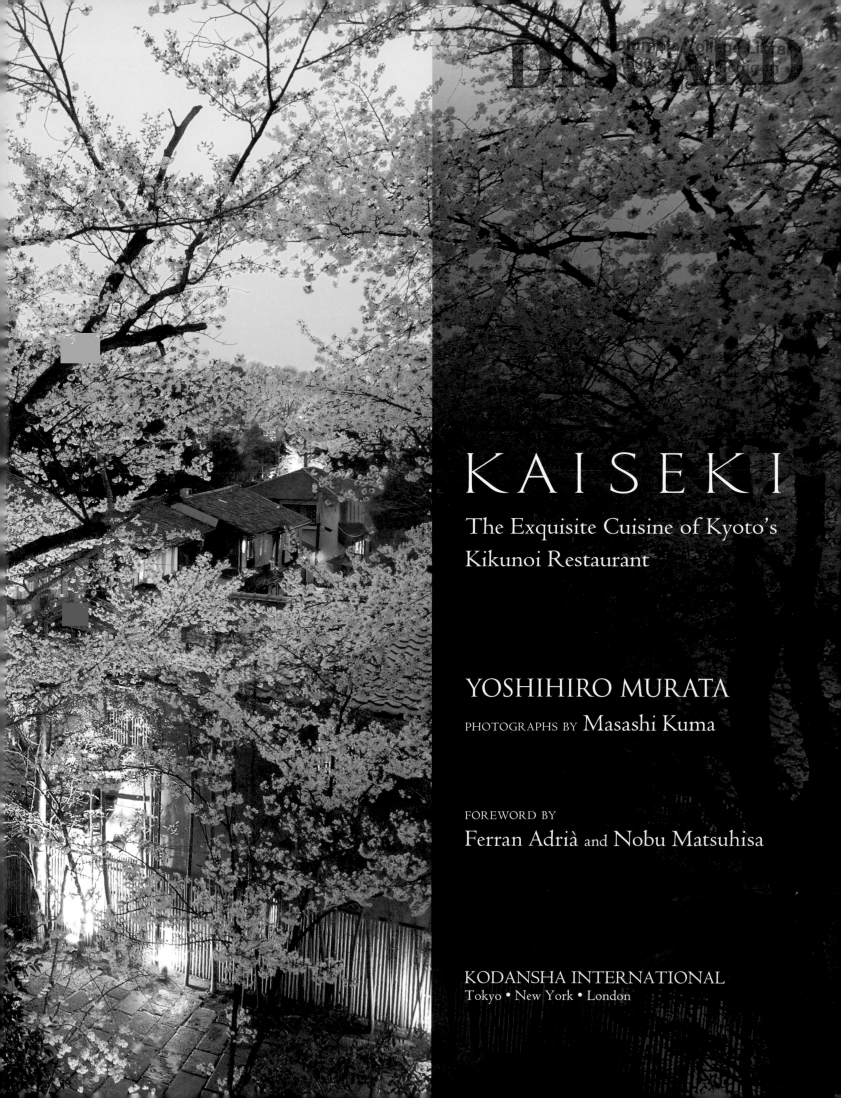

KAISEKI

The Exquisite Cuisine of Kyoto's
Kikunoi Restaurant

YOSHIHIRO MURATA

PHOTOGRAPHS BY Masashi Kuma

FOREWORD BY
Ferran Adrià and Nobu Matsuhisa

KODANSHA INTERNATIONAL
Tokyo • New York • London

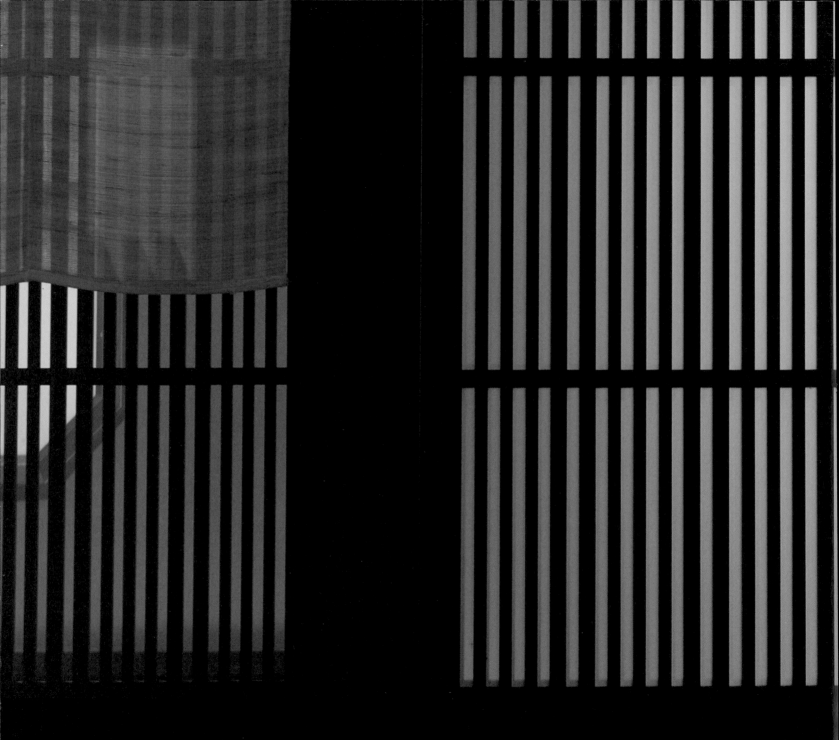

Distributed in the United States by Kodansha America Inc., and in the United Kingdom and continental Europe by Kodansha Europe Ltd.

Published by Kodansha International, Ltd., 17–14 Otowa 1-chome, Bunkyo-ku, Tokyo 112–8652, and Kodansha America, Inc.

Library of Congress Cataloging-in-Publication Data

Murata, Yoshihiro.
  Kaiseki : the exquisite cuisine of Kyoto's Kikunoi restaurant / by Yoshihiro Murata ; photographs by Masashi Kuma ; introduction by Ferran Adria and Nobuyuki Matsuhisa.

FOREWORD

When chef Yoshihiro Murata asked me to write a few words for this beautiful book, I saw it as the perfect opportunity to express my admiration for him in particular, and for Japanese cuisine in general. I have never made a secret of the fact that I believe Asian cuisine is one of the key innovative influences on Western haute cuisine. And amongst Asian cuisines, it is that of Japan that appeals to me most deeply—for its aesthetics, its philosophy, and its conceptual proximity to some of the dishes we offer from our own kitchen here at El Bulli. Also striking to me, as a Western chef, is the blend of traditional and modern elements that goes into the preparation of Japanese food.

I have always held that while in the West we cook with the senses, the heart, and logic, the Japanese add to this an extra component, one that is deeply anchored in their way of working and thinking: the soul. Nowhere is this better exemplified than by the work Yoshihiro Murata is carrying out at his magnificent restaurant, Kikunoi. I have many wonderful memories of my visits to Japan, but there are few places that have touched me on such a deep, spiritual level as Kyoto. It seems fitting that Kyoto should be the home of a cuisine, which, like the city itself, is born of an intimate communion between the work of man and the gifts of nature. This is what makes Yoshihiro Murata a truly unique chef.

Ferran Adrià
elBulli

Chef Yoshihiro Murata represents the best of a rarified area of Japanese cuisine: he has a firm commitment to traditional excellence along with a desire to always look for something fresh and innovative. Kaiseki cuisine has a long history but one of its great strengths is its flexibility—if anything, it incorporates the best of all styles of Japanese cooking. Though many Westerners prefer to dine from the same menu, regardless of the time of year, the true measure of the skill of a kaiseki chef is the way he prepares his meal in order to communicate the atmosphere and flavors of the season. He will carefully select everything from the elegant serving dishes to, say, a specific type of daikon radish that is only available at a certain time of year.

This book perfectly expresses the idea of, as I like to put it, "eating with one's eyes." Readers should get a sense of the importance Japanese chefs place on appearance, and Kikunoi is surely something special in this regard. And even though readers can't taste the food, I believe these photographs can stimulate the various senses—perhaps communicating the crunchiness of the skin of a grilled fish, or the seasonal "coolness" of a gelatin dish.

There may be much that is unfamiliar to readers who have yet to experience a kaiseki meal. But I firmly believe that will change as kaiseki becomes a word as comfortable and as familiar to food lovers worldwide as sushi, tempura and shabu shabu.

Nobu Matsuhisa
Nobu

INTRODUCTION

What is kaiseki?

The word *kaiseki* originally had little to do with cooking or tea. The *kai* means "bosom" and *seki* means "stone," and the term comes from the habit of monks in training to carry a heated stone in their robes, the warmth of which was intended to stave off hunger. Over the years, the word came to mean light meals to ward off the pangs of an empty stomach.

The cuisine's connection with tea began with Sen no Rikyu (1522–1591), the most renowned master of the tea ceremony. The high caffeine content of the powdered green tea was almost too intense to drink on an empty stomach, so tea ceremony practitioners began serving snacks to better enable guests to enjoy their tea. Rikyu's course was very simple at first—a bowl of miso soup and three side dishes—but the cooking became more elaborate as other side dishes were added.

Although the style of kaiseki created in restaurants like Kikunoi is based on Rikyu's philosophy, as chefs we must focus on our customers' enjoyment of the food, so the structure of our courses differs greatly from the tea master's. Today we distinguish between courses specifically for the tea ceremony—*cha-kaiseki*—and restaurant courses, known simply as kaiseki. There is another style, *Kyo-kaiseki*, based on Kyoto's traditional local cuisine, including *shojin-ryori* vegetarian temple food. In a city as small as Kyoto, of course, we have seen much overlapping of kaiseki and these local dishes, so I would have to say my meals are part of the Kyo-kaiseki tradition.

The Kikunoi Style

The ancestors to whom I trace the origins of Kikunoi were tea-ceremony practitioners who, in the early seventeenth century, accompanied the first wife of Regent Hideyoshi Toyotomi to Kyoto's Kodaiji Temple. They served there until around the time the Shogunate was overthrown in the 1868 Meiji Restoration, when the last ancestor of mine to work at the temple found himself abruptly out of a job. He only managed to survive by parlaying his kaiseki skills into the vocation of cook.

I am the third generation owner-chef of Kikunoi, which now consists of three establishments in Kyoto and Tokyo. Although I like to think of them all as *ryori-ya*, or simply, "restaurants," the

main restaurant, located in Kyoto's Gion Maruyama district, is strictly speaking a *ryotei*. The other Kyoto establishment features *kappo* cooking and the Tokyo restaurant falls somewhere between the two. My grandfather started the first one in 1912, but I must admit that my succession to the top position was not a smooth one—at least at first.

While still in college, I stunned my father by announcing that I would not follow him at the restaurant; that I wanted to cook French cuisine instead. His reaction was instant. "Then go to France. I'll take care of your expenses." It was my turn to be shocked since I had never thought about such a drastic move. My mother begged me to apologize to my father, but I knew I'd have to live with my rashness, and I left for France with no plans and a blank slate.

I managed to make some friends and find my way around. Later, I would visit one restaurant after the other in France and other countries as I traveled around Europe. It was an eye-opening experience and I learned to look at food in a much broader way, expanding my traditional ideas about methods and ingredients. Through my encounters with the cuisine of other cultures, I began to better appreciate Japanese food, and to understand that our cuisine is a product of our own DNA.

I returned to Japan after six months, and expressed my intentions of becoming a chef of Japanese cuisine to my father. But approval and a big welcome home wasn't in the cards. Instead, he acted furious at my change of heart and tossed a glass ashtray at me. (I still have the scar from that experience to remind me of his passion.)

My father also passed on to me several guiding principles that he had learned from my grandfather that would ensure that we would never lose the things that make us "Kikunoi." According to him, the food we make should always be refined and beautiful, but not too delicate. It should never be weak, but should have an appealing integrity and strength. And perhaps most importantly, he bid us to cook with love, technical skill and passion.

I still follow these principles whenever I have to make a decision. They are observed not only by me, but by everyone from the gardeners to all the craftsmen who work here. Thus we have been able to maintain our unique identity.

All these experiences have taught me that cooking is an evolutionary process that changes with time. Within the reliable, unchanging foundations of Kikunoi, I have been free to explore many forms of culinary expression, and I hope to continue to change and grow.

A Season to Eat

I believe that, in the end, kaiseki is all about enjoyment. So, as much as possible, I try to design every aspect of the experience to create a space and time where customers can relax and eat plenty of good food, take pleasure in the conversation, and leave feeling utterly satisfied. To give you a better idea of what's coming on the following pages, here are some notes about how the kaiseki courses work, using as an example the April menu from my flagship Kikunoi restaurant in Kyoto.

Once customers enter the restaurant and are seated in their private dining room, their first encounter with my cooking will be the *sakizuke*. Because there can only be one first impression, I take great care with this course. The ideal sakizuke is something that will put the customer at ease along with his or her first drink. The diner should feel no hesitation over digging in and finishing off the morsel in a couple of quick bites. I think the simple dish of sea bream milt fits the bill, evoking our delight over the new season.

The *hassun* is the second course, but it occupies the same place in the kaiseki meal as an overture holds in a symphony. I use an assortment of ingredients ranging from wild plants to seafood to establish the seasonal theme of the meal. The arrangement of the April hassun is meant to create a sense of picnicking among cherry blossoms.

Before any feelings of anticipation stirred by the hassun wane, I serve the *mukozuke*, which is an *otsukuri*, or sashimi dish. In April, as the main item in an assortment of sliced raw fish, I feature *sakura dai*, a pale-pink sea bream. Sashimi is a simple dish that spotlights the impeccable freshness of the fish and the knife skills of the cook, and the sakura dai is firmly associated with spring.

For the fourth course, the *futamono*, I serve a substantial dish for the first time. In April it is steamed Wakasa tilefish that perfumes the dining room with the gentle aroma of cherry blossoms. In cha-kaiseki this course would be a soup, but it is still early in the meal and I don't want to fill up my customers at this point.

In other months just one dish like smoked cherry salmon would be enough for the *yakimono* or grilled course. But *tofu dengaku* is an absolute must at rice-planting season, so I serve it as well. I take care not to prepare it too elaborately—it is best to rely on the clean, unadorned tastes of nature's seasonal bounty.

After the preceding full-flavored courses, for the *su-zakana*, I like to offer a rejuvenating cold dish mixed with dressing. I hope this wild vegetable salad evokes fresh mountain air. Over

the course of a meal, these kinds of refreshing dishes give the customer's palate a break.

This *shiizakana* course is usually the climax of the meal. In April my customers expect to be fed the culinary icon of spring: bamboo shoots. *Waka-take-ni* is a classic that almost everybody adores. At the same time, it is a very simple dish so I must pay special attention to its preparation, as it clearly demonstrates the cook's skill—or lack thereof.

I finish the main courses with *gohan,* rice or sushi mixed with various seasonal ingredients; *ko no mono,* homemade pickled vegetables; and *tome-wan,* a bowl of soup. If customers want steamed white rice, it is available as well.

The *mizumono,* April's dessert is a moderately sweet, chilled red bean soup. Even if customers think they are full, they can all enjoy this smooth and easy-to-eat dessert. Sometimes I serve traditional Japanese sweets, and other times I make ice cream or try some totally new flavor or ingredient. Serving dessert is one of my great pleasures as a chef.

So there you have it: a brief overview of the whys and hows of the kaiseki courses. As you can see, it is clearly a cuisine inextricably tied to the seasons. For whatever reason, modern Japanese have maintained their deep emotional linkage with the annual shifts in climate, ingrained from ancient times whether cultivating crops or fishing at the coast. So much is this connection the heart and soul of the cuisine, that when I am asked, "What is kaiseki?" I often have a very simple answer.

"It is eating the seasons."

Yoshihiro Murata

The gorgeous three-dimensional objects in the decorative gold-leafing called *kirikane* which grace the seasonal chapter openings are the works of Sayoko Eri, a Kyoto artist who has been honored as a Living National Treasure of Japan.

KAISEKI COURSES

Sakizuke 先付

The first course is also called *tsukidashi* or *otoshi*, the equivalent of an *amuse-gueule* in French cuisine.

Hassun 八寸

The second course sets the seasonal theme and consists of one kind of sushi and five or six small side dishes, sometimes served in the middle courses.

Mukozuke 向付

The third course is usually an *Otsukuri*, or sliced dish, of seasonal sashimi.

Takiawase 煮合

A medley or vegetables and fish, meat, or tofu, simmered separately.

Futamono 蓋物

A substantial dish, usually *nimono-wan*, often a hearty soup, but not always. Futamono means a lidded dish.

Yakimono 焼物

Usually a broiled seasonal fish. Sometimes tofu, bamboo shoots, or eggplant are served as yakimono.

Su-zakana 酢肴

Served to refresh the palate, usually comprised of crisply textured vegetables and wild plants in a mildly sour vinegar dressing.

Hiyashi-bachi 冷し鉢

A chilled dish served only during summer, made of assorted simmered vegetables.

Naka-choko 中猪口

Another palate refresher, a very light dish such as *tomato no suri nagashi* chilled tomato soup.

Shiizakana 強肴

In restaurant kaiseki courses, the *shiizakana* could be assorted simmered, dressed, or hot pot dishes.

Gohan 御飯

Cooked rice with seasonal ingredients or mixed sushi, *iimushi* steamed glutinous rice or *donburi* topped rice dishes could also be served.

Ko no mono 香の物

Seasonal home-pickled vegetables, for example, rapini in spring, cucumber or eggplant in summer, etc.

Tome-wan 止椀

Soup served with rice and *ko no mono*. Traditionally a miso based soup but now is often a seasonal vegetable potage.

Mizumono 水物

A seasonal dessert chosen from among nostalgic sweets, Japanese confections and original ice cream or cakes.

SPRING

隠れ梅
Kakure Ume

HIDDEN UME

As March begins, the sweet-smelling Japanese plum blossoms called *ume no hana* have nearly finished blooming. I especially enjoy viewing these blossoms as the year's final snowflakes quietly fall. The vibrant pink flowers covered in pallid snow make for a breathtaking tableau of transient beauty. I wanted to reflect this fleeting loveliness in my cooking.

To recreate such an image on a plate I cover large, tart pink *umeboshi*, or pickled plums, with a sauce made of *shirako*, the pristine white milt of sea bream. After leaching the salt from the plums, I simmer them in light *dashi* and leave them to cool slowly. For the sauce I steam exquisitely fresh sea bream milt with sake and force it through a fine sieve. Then I mix toasted and ground sesame seeds, *atari goma*, with the milt to create a smooth cream, the thickness of which I adjust with dashi. Finally I season with light soy sauce, salt and *mirin*. The shirako cream must be less salty than the umeboshi, or the dish doesn't work. What lies at the bottom should be more heavily seasoned, and what's on top should be lighter. This balance is very important.

The mild, fragrant pickled plums harmonize with the rich and smooth *shirako* cream to create a dish I look forward to every March.

先付　**March *Sakizuke***

- *Umeboshi*/pickled plums ∙ *tai no shirako*/sea bream milt
- *atari goma*/toasted ground sesame seeds
- *tsukushi*/horsetail shoots　*recipe p.163*

卯月の八寸　*Uzuki no Hassun*

APRIL HASSUN

I like to think of Kikunoi as an amusement park for adults. It's where my customers can relax, enjoy some respite from the daily grind, and partake in a culinary adventure. After I've got their attention with the sakizuke, I try to build on that momentum in the next course—the hassun—which is key to setting the theme for the evening. I create a vignette of each month, sketching in the details with seasonal provender. On serving a dish, I feel a rush of satisfaction if my customers say, "Wow, that is gorgeous." The theme of our April hassun is *o-hanami*: cherry-blossom viewing. I want to evoke a feeling of picnicking under cherry trees on a regal, crimson carpet, while watching the delicate pink petals flutter elegantly to earth.

鯛木の芽寿司　*Tai Kinome-zushi*
SEA BREAM AND KINOME SUSHI
A stick of sushi made from vinegared sea bream and *Shiroita kombu*, atop sushi rice flecked with peppery fragments of *kinome* buds

花弁独活　*Hanabira Udo*
PETAL-SHAPED UDO
Cherry-blossom-shaped slices of *udo* stalk

花見団子　*Hanami Dango*
DUMPLINGS FOR CHERRY-BLOSSOM VIEWING
A panache of shrimp, avocado and abalone skewered to resemble *hanami dango*—rice dumplings eaten while blossom viewing

花弁百合根　*Hanabira Yurine*
LILY BULB PETALS
Steamed petal-shaped pieces of lily bulb topped with seasoned salmon roe

飯蛸　*Iidako*
SMALL OCTOPUS
Roe-filled baby octopus cooked with a touch of sugar

一寸豆　*Issun Mame*
BROAD BEANS
Boiled *soramame*, small broad beans

蕨烏賊　*Warabi Ika*
BROILED SQUID
Squid skewered to resemble *warabi* bracken fern, broiled and dusted with dried green *nori* seaweed powder

蝶々長芋　*Chocho Nagaimo*
BUTTERFLY CHINESE YAMS
Slices of Chinese yams punched into butterfly-shapes, simmered in lightly seasoned dashi and covered with crumbled egg yolk.

recipes p.163

若狭ぐじ桜蒸し
Wakasa Guji Sakura-mushi

STEAMED WAKASA TILEFISH WITH CHERRY BLOSSOMS

Wakasa tilefish has long been a staple of Kyoto cuisine. Diners enjoy its delicate taste and chefs are grateful for the nearly blank canvas it provides for their culinary efforts. Our April *futamono* features tilefish in a dish with a cherry blossom motif. I've wrapped thin slices of the fish around steamed, crushed glutinous rice that has been flavored with salt-preserved cherry blossoms. This little package is covered with a salted cherry-tree leaf and after being steamed, is enrobed in a sauce made from thickened bonito stock.

When customers lift the lid of the bowl, the scent of cherry blossoms rises on the steam, echoing the fragrance of cherry trees in full bloom. This wafting aroma is critical to the success of the dish. I've often admired the way French or Italian chefs use herbs, sometimes with a delicate hand and other times boldly. It adds a distinctive signature to their dishes. The fragrance of Japanese cuisine is always very subdued. This is fine, but I contend there is also nothing wrong with serving gorgeously perfumed dishes.

蓋物 April *Futamono*

- **Wakasa tilefish** ■ *domyoji/***ground glutinous rice**
- **salted cherry-tree leaves** ■ **salted cherry blossoms**
- *warabi/***bracken** ■ *gin-an/***thickened sauce** ■ **ginger juice**
- *bubu arare/***tiny rice crackers** *recipe p.164*

鯛白子酒蒸し *Tai Shirako Saka-mushi*

SAKE-STEAMED SEA BREAM MILT

The orange puree in this dish is *nama konoko*, fresh sea cucumber roe, a delicacy whose aroma captures the very essence of the sea. The white glossy portion is an intensely flavored sea bream milt steamed with sake. Sea cucumber and sea bream spawn only once a year, in spring, so their roe and milt are available only fleetingly. The ingredients are very delicate and must be eaten at the peak of freshness. The same goes for the garnish, a frail spring orchid blossom called *shunran*.

Bringing together these exquisite and rare ingredients, preparing them impeccably and arranging them on the plate that suits them best is my way of telling customers, "Thanks for coming." This sort of attention to detail and the moment, which is at the heart of hospitality, is expressed in the saying: *"Ichigo ichie,"* which means, "Treasure every meeting, for it will never happen again."

先付 April *Sakizuke*

- *Tai shirako/***sea bream milt** ■ *konoko/***fresh sea cucumber roe**
- *shunran/***spring orchid flowers** ■ *pon-zu/***citrus vinegar** *recipe p.164*

蛍烏賊と山菜土佐酢和え
Hotaru Ika to Sansai Tosa-zu-ae

VINEGARED FIREFLY SQUID AND WILD VEGETABLES

The crisp texture of edible wild mountain vegetables with their distinctive green fragrance combines well with the sweetness of tiny whole *hotaru ika* (firefly squid) in April's su-zakana. A light touch of mild *Tosa-zu* vinegar jelly provides a simple dressing for this rustic dish. Edible wild plants like *kogomi*, *fuki*, and *yama udo* are some of the first vegetables to burst forth in the spring. We hope that by eating them we can absorb some of the season's youthful vigor.

A little signature touch is the use of Tosa-zu jelly instead of the standard liquid Tosa-zu. I add just a dab of gelatin and when it hardens I strain it. If it were a liquid, it would just run off, but this delicate jelly sticks to the other ingredients. It is a good technique to use with a sauce that is slightly sour or salty.

The bowl is in the Shigaraki style; earthy and rugged, it provides a perfect stage for these rustic mountain vegetables.

酢肴 April *Su-zakana*

- *Hotaru ika*/firefly squid ▪ *kogomi* ▪ *fuki* ▪ *yama udo*
- *Tosa-zu jelly* ▪ *kinome*/Japanese pepper leaf buds *recipe p.164*

御造り
Otsukuri

Sashimi

真鯛 *Madai*

RED SEA BREAM

Cutting techniques are an essential element of Japanese cuisine, and the word *otsukuri* encompasses the entire process of creating a course by cutting. Proper technique is needed to make cuts that are clean—with sharp edges and glossy surfaces. Without such skills, no one can create *sashimi*. Technique also derives from one's instruments: the Western-style knife has a double cutting edge that forcefully divides items in two, whereas the Japanese knife is single-edged, like a carpenter's chisel, and easily slides into the object being cut, then glides through smoothly. To slice fish for sashimi, I angle the knife against the fish and maintain this angle as I draw the blade toward myself, using the weight of the knife and the entire length of the blade to make the cut.

In Kyoto cuisine, we prefer white-fleshed fish, especially sea bream. It is difficult to imagine Kyoto cooking without it. We treasure it so much that we even have a special name for each month's bream. For example, in April the fish is *sakura dai*, cherry-blossom sea bream, in May it is *satsuki dai*, May sea bream, and in June it is called *mugiwara dai*, or barley-field sea bream, since in June the barley is up.

向付 Spring *Mukozuke*

■ *Madai*/red sea bream ■ grated *wasabi* ■ Tosa soy sauce
recipe p.164

赤貝 *Akagai*

ARK SHELLS

The condiments that accompany the *otsukuri* must be carefully chosen as it is a simple dish and they can strongly influence its taste.

The soy sauce I serve with sashimi at my restaurant is "real soy sauce," produced at an old brewery where beneficial yeasts and molds have long colonized the building, and a wooden brewing tank has been in use for over one hundred years. Following time-honored methods, the brewers use only high-quality, whole soybeans grown in Japan, wheat, and sea salt, to slowly brew the sauce. To make *Tosa-joyu* seasoned soy sauce, I heat sake that has had its alcohol burned off with the soy sauce to dilute its strength. When the mixture

boils I add dried bonito flakes then let it cool before filtering. If the sauce is too strong, it will overwhelm the sashimi, so I make it as mild as possible. The aroma and piquancy of grated wasabi goes well with this mild Tosa sauce. Sometimes I add a squeeze of *sudachi* juice to liven it up.

We obtain our *akagai* ark shells from the Kochi district of Shikoku. The meat has a firm but yielding texture and a vibrant color. It is most crisp and delicious when eaten within ten minutes of removal from its shell.

向付 **Spring *Mukozuke***

■ *Akagai*/ark shells ■ grated *wasabi* ■ Tosa soy sauce

recipe p.164

SEA BREAM SUSHI WRAPPED IN BAMBOO LEAVES

We celebrate the Boys' Festival on the fifth of May with *kashiwa mochi*, a sweet rice cake wrapped in an oak leaf, and *chimaki*, another kind of rice cake wrapped in bamboo leaves. Continuing the tradition, each May I serve *chimaki zushi* as part of the *hassun* selection. The chimaki's sushi rice is made from a mix of regular and glutinous rice. I season the rice with some peppery *kinome* leaf buds for a lively taste.

The sea bream fillet is briefly marinated in *shime-zu* (vinegar) and then sliced. To make each one, I cover a cylindrical piece of rice with a slice of the marinated fish, wrap it in bamboo leaves and tie with gold and silver colored string. When I unwrap the *chimaki*, its green bamboo leaf aroma lets me know that summer is almost here.

Chimaki is an interesting food of myriad shapes and ingredients, depending on the region. Not too long ago, everybody used to make them at home. Nobody seems to have time for this anymore, so our restaurant can play an important role in preserving these traditional foodways.

八寸 **May Hassun**

■ **Sushi rice** ■ **glutinous rice** ■ *tai* **sea bream**
■ *kinome*/**Japanese pepper leaf buds**
■ **bamboo leaves** *recipe p.165*

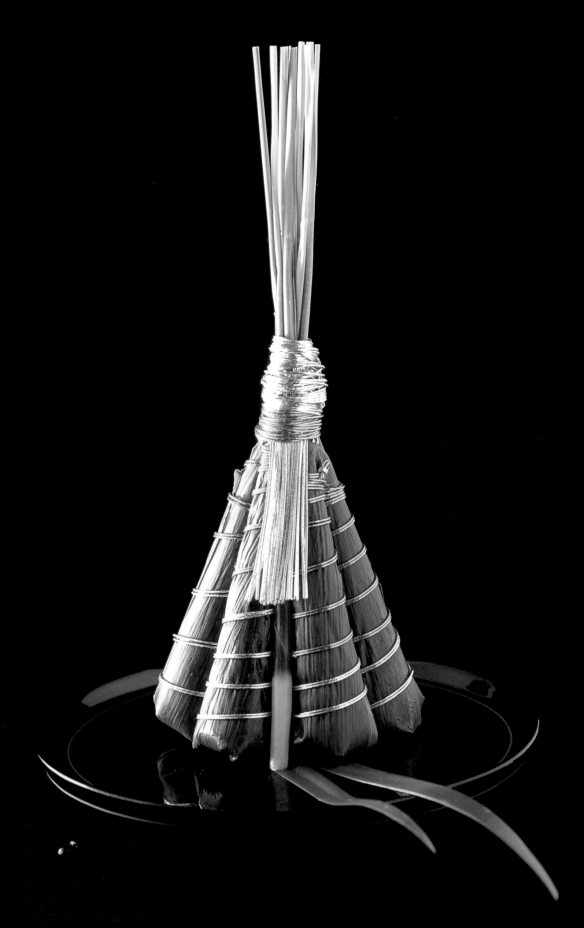

桜鱒燻し焼き
Sakura Masu Ibushi-yaki

SMOKED CHERRY SALMON

In my thirties, I published a book titled *Kyo Ryori Kara: Konnan Umai, Konnan Sukiya* (Cuisine From Kyoto: What's Good and What I Like). I wrote it as a reevaluation of the traditions of Kyoto cuisine, and I wanted to show the public what I was up to in the kitchen—and hopefully learn what they thought about it.

One of the dishes in the book was *Sawara no Ibushi-yaki* (smoked Spanish mackerel). I wondered why there weren't any smoked dishes in Kyoto cuisine. We use dried bonito flakes—which are smoked—and broiled fish certainly is no stranger to the scent of charcoal. I thought a rich, full-bodied fish like sawara would work well with smoke. Before smoking the sawara I marinated it in *yuanji* for a distinctive Kyoto touch.

Nowadays, cherry salmon caught in Toyama Prefecture on the Japan Sea coast is my favored fish for smoking. As the name indicates, its flesh is pink like a cherry blossom. After marinating in miso yuanji, I skewer the fish and lightly broil it before smoking it over cherry wood. I'm always thrilled if my customers can enjoy this culinary homage to spring while the cherry trees are still in bloom.

焼物　April *Yakimono*

■ **Cherry salmon** ■ *miso yuanji*/**miso marinade** ■ *kinome*/**Japanese pepper leaf buds**　*recipe p.165*

穴子東寺巻き
Anago Toji-maki

SEA EEL AND YUBA ROLLS

Toji-maki is a spring favorite made with fresh *yuba* soy skin. It takes its name from To-ji (East Temple), which was built over 1200 years ago during the Heian period. To-ji was on the east side of the Rashomon, the gate and location made famous by film director Akira Kurosawa. The gate of cinematic renown is long gone, but the temple still functions as a place of worship. The Buddhist monks there were vegetarians and their special *shojin-ryori* often included tofu or yuba. They would roll a variety of ingredients in soy skin and deep-fry them. At Kikunoi we wrap seasoned *anago* (sea eel) in thin sheets of *hikiage* yuba, deep-fry them, then simmer in a light *dashi*. Yuba soaks up the sea eel's flavor from within, and the oil and dashi from without, making for a very savory dish.

Freshness is crucial for raw yuba and my local shop will send over just five or ten sheets by scooter as soon as I order— a great help. Unlike other parts of Japan, in Kyoto there are separate stores that sell only yuba, or just tofu. The demand in Kyoto is high enough to keep both kinds of shops in business.

煮合 **March Takiawase**

■ *Anago*/sea eel ■ *hikiage nama yuba*/Fresh soy-milk skin ■ dried *shiitake* mushrooms ■ *hatakena*/mustard greens ■ julienned *yuzu*

recipe p.165

若狭ぐじ雲丹焼き
Wakasa Guji Uni-yaki

TILEFISH GRILLED WITH SEA URCHIN ROE

Every year on March third we celebrate the *Hina Matsuri*, or Dolls' Festival. It is a special day for girls so I wanted to make a *yakimono*, a grilled dish, as cute as a doll. This tilefish grilled with sea urchin roe may look man-sized in the photograph, but it is actually so petite you could finish it off in a couple of bites.

To make the dish, I marinate Wakasa tilefish in *Saikyo miso* paste. I want it to be very rich so I cut thick slices of fish. When the fish is suffused with the sweet miso's flavor, I broil it over charcoal. Then I cover it with sea urchin roe and a little rock salt, and quickly brown the top. It looks like a tartlet of tilefish and sea urchin roe. The tilefish is so soft that it melts in your mouth, while the sea urchin roe is raw, sweet and marvelously creamy. The salt adds a counterpoint to this sweet harmony. Before you realize it, one piece is gone, then another. Suddenly there is nothing left but a yearning for another bite. I like to serve a tantalizing tidbit of something rich that leaves my customers wanting more.

焼物 March *Yakimono*

- **Wakasa tilefish** ▪ **sea urchin roe** ▪ *Saikyo miso* **paste**
- *fuki no to*/**coltsfoot buds** *recipe p.165*

豆腐田楽
Tofu Dengaku

BROILED TOFU WITH MISO PASTE

Dengaku was originally music and dance offered to the gods of the harvest at rice-planting season. A square of tofu on a skewer reminded people of a dengaku performer with a pole, so this broiled tofu dish came to be called dengaku. Later the name came to encompass *sato-imo*—a kind of taro—and eggplant which were dipped in *miso* paste and grilled. Dengaku dishes have evolved over the years and nowadays almost anything slathered with miso and broiled might be called dengaku, regardless of whether it is skewered.

At Kikunoi we stay loyal to the origins of the dish and serve tofu skewered on a green bamboo stick. Making an old-fashioned standard is quite different from inventing a new dish, but I try to put a Kikunoi spin on the classics too. I use a very soft tofu that is difficult to skewer and melts in your mouth like custard. The miso topping is seasoned with a substantial amount of spicy *kinome* buds. Before serving, it is important to lightly scorch the topping to release its toasty fragrance.

焼物 *April Yakimono*

■ **Tofu** ■ **white miso paste** ■ **eggs**
■ *kinome*/**Japanese pepper leaf buds** *recipe p.165*

筍寿司
Takenoko-zushi

BAMBOO SHOOT SUSHI

My grandfather, the first owner of Kikunoi, adored bamboo shoots. While waiting for the unearthing of the first shoots of spring, he would ponder aloud the best way to prepare them. Bamboo shoots are one of those foods that people anticipate gleefully each year. Every country has these seasonal delicacies; in France they are crazy about the year's first tender asparagus spears. Tossed with soft-boiled eggs or sprinkled with good olive oil and salt, they are simply fantastic.

In Kyoto in April, my customers definitely expect to be fed bamboo shoots. They arrive thinking: "Today's rice must be cooked with bamboo shoots." I throw them a little curve and offer bamboo shoot sushi. I combine *abura age* (deep-fried tofu), bamboo shoots, and *jako* (tiny dried fish), soaked in seasoned vinegar. The sushi rice is steamed with a little glutinous rice and the deep-fried tofu brings out the best in the bamboo shoots. I mince the tofu until it is barely noticeable. The bamboo's crunchy texture is still prominent even after it has been chopped into small bits.

御飯 April *Gohan*

■ Bamboo shoots ■ sushi rice ■ *chirimen jako*/tiny dried fish
■ *kinome*/Japanese pepper leaf buds
■ *ko no mono* (*kombu, daikon, nanohana* rape blossoms and *hajikami* pickled ginger shoots)/pickles *recipe p.165*

焼き筍
Yaki Takenoko

BAKED BAMBOO SHOOTS

"Here's one! . . . And look, another one over there."

"Really? Where is it?" I can't see what he's talking about, but when young Mr. Murakami turns the soil with his long, slim hoe, a new bamboo shoot suddenly materializes. I ask: "How can you tell where they are?"

"Because the soil is swollen," he replies.

Mr. Murakami has a trained eye. He lives in a nearby farmhouse and has been harvesting bamboo shoots in this area for a long time. In spring, the shoots grow on underground stems that spread throughout the grove. The harvest lasts just one month. During the year he tends the grove, thinning the bamboo and mulching with straw. The fragrant shoots grow white and delicious in the fertile earth. Bamboo shoots begin to get bitter as soon as they are dug up.

To stop them from getting even more bitter, we blanch them in boiling water as soon as they arrive in the kitchen. To serve, I roast them in a 350°F/180°C oven for about fifteen minutes. I brown the surface and cut them into bite-size pieces then rush them into the dining room while they are still piping hot.

I hope that with their first bite my customers will be whisked to that quiet bamboo grove where, only this morning, the shoots were growing.

焼物 **April** *Yakimono*

- **Bamboo shoots** ▪ *kinome*/**Japanese pepper leaf buds**
▪ **leaf bud miso paste** *recipe p.166*

若竹煮
Waka-take-ni

WAKAME AND BAMBOO SHOOTS

Waka-take-ni is one of those classics that never seem to change. It feels only natural every spring to simmer delicate green *wakame* seaweed with crisp bamboo shoots. I deviate slightly from the standard recipe with the addition of sea bream ovaries. It seems to belong there and these ingredients combine easily to create a savory three-part harmony. I simmer the bite-size pieces of bamboo shoots in seasoned *dashi* fortified with the addition of dried bonito flakes wrapped in gauze. Then I leave the shoots to cool in the stock. Sea bream ovaries are cooked separately in a slightly sweet stock. My wakame is harvested from under a whirlpool in the Naruto Channel, where the dynamic action of the swirling ocean gives it a unique texture that is soft but crisp. I use salted wakame because it has more flavor than the fresh type.

The serving bowl was fashioned 500 years ago in Korea during the Choson dynasty. It has a sublime strength and simplicity that is perfectly suited to this classic dish of bamboo shoots.

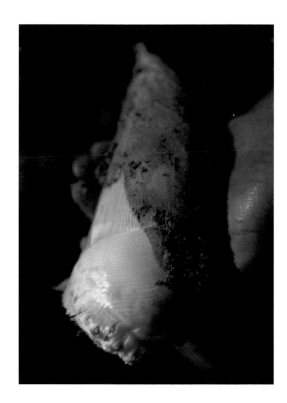

強肴 April *Shiizakana*

■ Bamboo shoots ■ *wakame*/seaweed ■ sea bream ovaries
■ *kinome*/Japanese pepper leaf buds *recipe p.166*

海老真丈鶯仕立て

Ebi Shinjo Uguisu-jitate

PEA SOUP WITH SHRIMP BALLS

Traditionally, miso soup is served as *Tome-wan*, the soup that comes at the close of the kaiseki course. I wanted to serve something lighter-tasting that would satisfy diners seeking a healthier diet. At my main restaurant, Kikunoi, I now serve both vegetable potage and miso soup depending on the courses. However, at the Roan branch (also in Kyoto) and the Akasaka branch in Tokyo, the tome-wan is exclusively made with seasonal vegetables. For example, in March the potage might be spinach, young cabbage in May, onions in June, *edamame* green soybeans in July, and so on.

April's tome-wan is made from a velvety puree of green peas garnished with fried shrimp balls. The cooking method is very simple but care must be taken to preserve the peas' vibrant green color. The peas can only be heated twice—once before pureeing and once just before serving. A third time on the fire and their color and aroma will vanish.

As for the shrimp balls, I deep-fry them; that way they are brown on the outside and reveal their pink interior when cut with chopsticks. It's a little more interesting than just putting pink shrimp balls into a green soup.

止椀 April *Tome-wan*

■ **Green peas** ■ **shrimp** ■ **ground fish** ■ **yams** ■ **black sesame seeds**
■ *hanabira udo*/**udo cut into petal-shapes** *recipe p. 166*

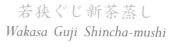

STEAMED TILEFISH WITH FRESH GREEN TEA LEAVES

Uji city, near Kyoto, has a long history of growing some of Japan's finest tea. The year's first leaves are harvested throughout May, which gave me the inspiration for this month's dish. The owner of a tea shop in Uji told me that his customers enjoyed nibbling on fresh leaves of select, shade-grown *gyokuro* tea as they sipped their tea. In this dish, I have elaborated on the traditional recipe of tilefish steamed with green tea noodles, called *shinshu-mushi*, by adding a topping of fresh *gyokuro* leaves and infusing the usual bonito broth with tea, which creates a flavor both novel and profound.

The lidded serving bowl features a flamboyant low-fire glaze over three-dimensional designs. The selection of plates and bowls is an important part of kaiseki. I choose them to suit the food, and I also take care to create a rhythm by alternating austere, sophisticated ceramics with sumptuous pieces throughout the meal. I want the variety of the serving ware to enhance the patrons' enjoyment of their meal.

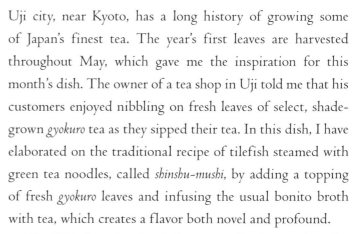

蓋物 **May** *Futamono*

■ Wakasa tilefish ■ *cha-soba*/green tea noodles ■ *gyokuro* tea leaves
■ thin omlet ■ *tsuyu* soup (*bonito* stock, light soy sauce,
regular soy sauce and mirin) ■ sliced green onions
■ *momiji oroshi*/radish grated with chili peppers
■ julienned nori   *recipe p.166*

散らし寿司
Chirashi-zushi

SCATTERED SPRING SUSHI

Every year I look forward to making *chirashi-zushi* in March. I always imagine a warm day in spring where I throw myself down and stretch out on a bed of fresh young grass. Glancing about, I can see all kinds of plants budding and various shoots reaching for the sun. A single early cherry blossom petal sails by on the wind. Taking a deep breath, I am filled with fresh green scent and without realizing it, I begin to feel at peace. That's the scene I want to evoke with this chirashi.

Kaiseki chirashi differs from the type served at sushi bars in that we do not use raw seafood at all. That is an important difference. Since we serve *otsukuri* (sashimi) in the *mukozuke* course, we can't use it again in the rice course. The rice provides a foundation for fourteen different ingredients. Each one is cooked separately, but even with all the flavors mixed together, the individual components are still distinct. Every bite yields a unique taste.

御飯 **March Gohan**

■ **Chirashi-zushi** *(see recipe on page 167 for ingredients)*

春の水物 *Haru no Mizumono*

SPRING MIZUMONO

Sometimes I am floored by my customers' comments. "It seems a pity to serve just a couple of pieces of fruit as *mizumono*," said one, "after all those elaborate dishes." The thought had never occurred to me; I had always accepted that mizumono must be composed of seasonal fruit. But this remark made me decide to serve something more imaginative, and my repertoire of sweets has expanded greatly.

Customers certainly like my *kusa mochi*—a popular spring dessert. Every Japanese is familiar with it, and it is available at any confectioner. It is comprised of chewy, sweet rice cakes, colored and scented with bright green mugwort. The filling is sweet, mashed red beans, and the cakes make the perfect foil for a cup of green tea. Of course, it puts extra pressure on me to serve this kind of everyday item but I enjoy the challenge of improving on an old standard. The aroma of mugwort in the dumplings is strong, and the color is green as jade.

I also serve *annin-dofu*, a milk pudding flavored with apricot kernel and almond powder. I've heard this Chinese pudding was the inspiration for blancmange. I make this dessert so smooth and delicate that it almost disintegrates when it hits your tongue. It has a strong, sweet, marzipan-like fragrance, and for a stylish touch I add a garnish of gelatinous Thai basil seeds.

草餅 *Kusa Mochi*
GREEN RICE CAKES WITH RED BEAN PASTE
- **Yomogi/mugwort** ■ **rice flour** ■ **sweet red-bean paste**
- **kinako/soybean powder** *recipe p.168*

杏仁豆腐 *Annin-dofu*
ALMOND JELLY
- **Annin/Chinese apricot kernel powder** ■ **almond powder** ■ **milk**
- **gelatin** ■ **syrup** ■ **Thai basil seeds** *recipe p.168*

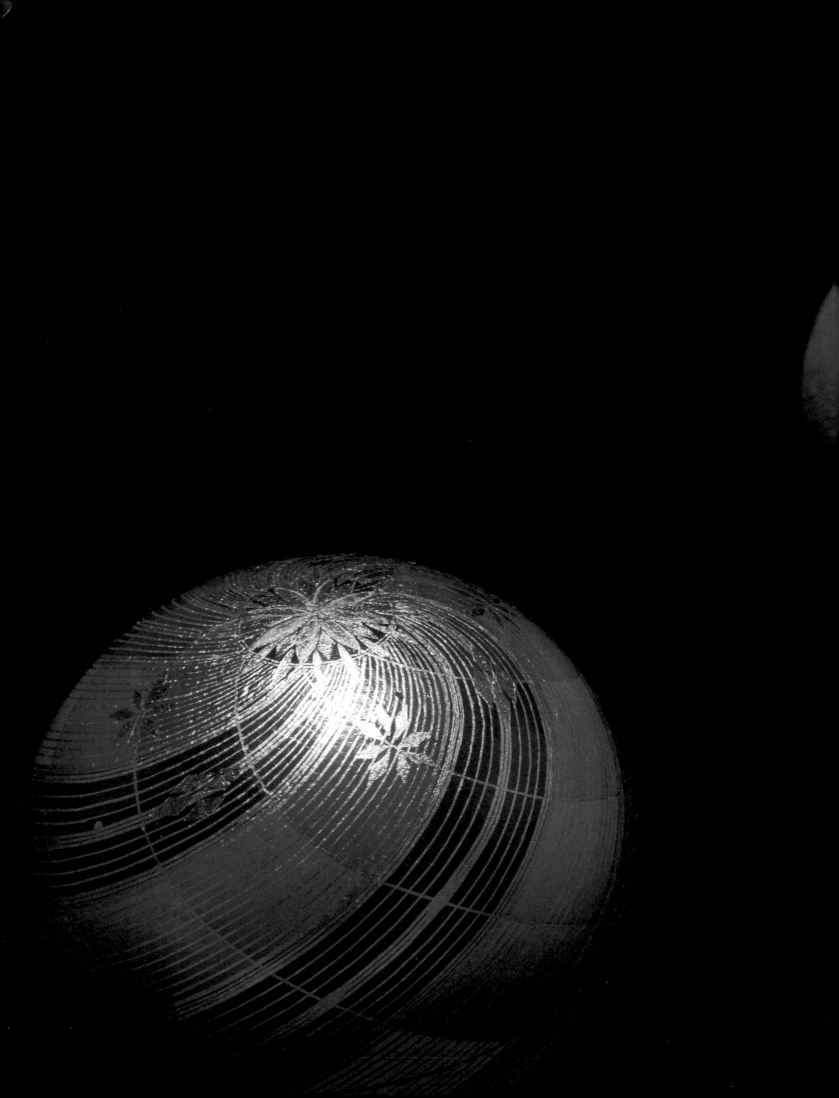

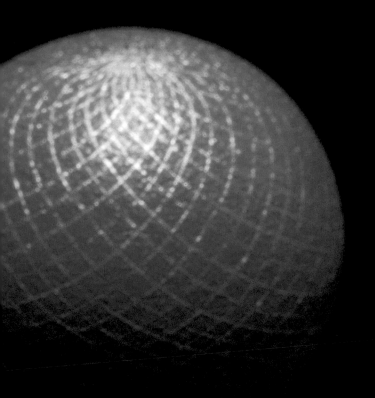

SUMMER

文月の八寸　*Fumizuki no Hassun*

JULY HASSUN

If you visit Kyoto in July there is no escaping the festival that is *Gion Matsuri*. The entire town bubbles with energy. Lanterns light the streets, and the irresistible rhythms of carnival music, called *konchikichin*, crank up the excitement. In a peaceful ritual, we hang amulets made of bamboo leaves and paper on our front gates to protect us from evil in the coming year. On the paper are written the words "We are descendants of Somin Shorai." Legend has it that Somin Shorai was a poor man who offered food and lodging to a rather shabby-looking god, and was rewarded with a magic ring of grass that warded off plague, thus saving him and his family. In keeping with the legend, I decorate July's *hassun* with a bamboo leaf and attach a small piece of paper on which is written the message of Somin Shorai. There is so much hoopla surrounding the Gion festival that this small touch is enough to underline July's theme.

鱧寿司　*Hamo-zushi*
HAMO SUSHI
A stick of sushi topped with broiled *hamo* and painted with a sweet and salty sauce

薑　*Hajikami*
PICKLED GINGER SHOOTS
Blanched ginger shoots soaked in plum vinegar

利休麩と青瓜雷干し翡翠和え
Rikyu-fu to Aouri Kaminari-boshi Hisui-ae
RIKYU-FU AND SALTED GREEN GOURD
Cooked *Rikyu-fu*, a kind of wheat gluten common in meatless temple cuisine, and wilted green gourd with *Tosa-zu* vinegar and grated cucumber

鼈甲生薑　*Bekko Shoga*
AMBER GINGER
Caramelized young ginger roots

川海老　*Kawa Ebi*
RIVER SHRIMP
Lightly seasoned boiled river shrimp

蛸の子　*Tako no Ko*
OCTOPUS ROE
Simmered octopus roe in lightly seasoned dashi

若狭ぐじ胡瓜巻き　*Wakasa Guji Kyuri-maki*
TILEFISH ROLL WITH CUCUMBER
Tilefish and cucumber wrapped around a refreshing core of julienned ginger seasoned with sugar and vinegar

recipes p.168

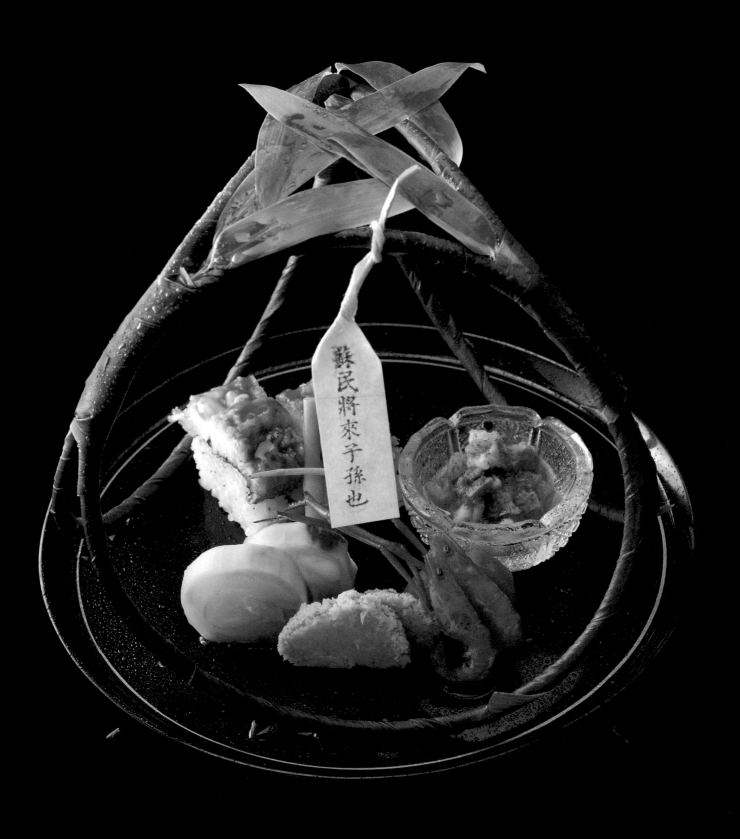

青梅白ワイン煮
Aoume Shiro-wine-ni

GREEN JAPANESE PLUMS IN WHITE WINE

Come June every year, I can't help but gaze rapt at the beauty of green Japanese plums (*Prunus mume*). Their emerald color is so vivid they seem to pulse with life. Green plum *kanro-ni*, sweetened green plums, is a traditional dish. The classic cooking method involves blanching them to remove their sourness, then simmering in very sweet syrup. I find the sour taste to be a fundamental characteristic of plums, so when I first attempted this dish I tried leaving them mildly sour, and coaxing out more of their fruity fragrance, by using less sugar. To further boost the aroma I used a splash of white wine. I found the taste to be perfect, but the beautiful green color had paled in the cooking process. Then I recalled something my father had told me: simply cook them in a copper pot. I took his advice and the plums retained their vivid hue. My father was a man of few words, who passed away thirteen years ago, but I always remember him fondly when I cook this dish.

To imitate rain drops, I top the plums with ice made from the simmering syrup. The skin has softened to insubstantiality, and the pulp is tender, fragrant and both sweet and sour. Although in reality fresh picked green plums are too hard, sour and bitter to eat, I want this dish to conjure the fantasy of eating dewy, fresh green plums in the orchard.

The serving dish is old Baccarat crystal.

先付 June *Sakizuke*

Green Japanese plums ■ white wine ■ granulated sugar
recipe p.169

無花果西京煮
Ichijiku Saikyo-ni

FIGS SIMMERED IN WHITE MISO

I spend a fair amount of time pondering which cooking method is best for a particular dish, or how I might meld certain ingredients into a more harmonious whole. Often the solutions to these conundrums come more easily when I simply approach an ingredient from a different angle.

Take the fig, for example. Here is a fruit that is not terribly sweet; in fact, when green it tastes almost like a vegetable. I treat it as such and simmer it with a mildly sweet *Saikyo miso*, which highlights the contrast between the austerity of the green fig and the rich miso's mild sweetness.

When I was young, I thought it was my job to always add another taste dimension to every ingredient. But these days I find that approach a little arrogant. The real work of the chef is to coax out the fundamental taste that is innate to any ingredient. To that end, in this dish I used a less assertive bonito stock, to bring out the fresh juiciness and subtle cinnamon fragrance of the cooked fig.

先付 **August** *Sakizuke*

■ **Green figs** ■ *Saikyo miso* ■ **fine bonito flakes**
■ **Japanese mustard** *recipe p.169*

トマト擂り流し
Tomato Suri-nagashi

CHILLED TOMATO SOUP

This stunning scarlet dish was inspired by an absolutely perfect tomato I sampled at the farmhouse where I always buy my fresh local produce in Kami-gamo, northern Kyoto.

To make this refreshing summer soup, I first crush the tomatoes and strain them through a fine bamboo sieve. To concentrate the tomato flavor, I simmer half of the juice until it gets good and thick. After cooling, the thickened puree is brightened by the addition of the remaining uncooked juice. The seasoning is simplicity itself: a pinch of salt, a dash of light soy sauce and lemon juice. A smooth topping comprised of fresh *kumiage yuba* (a delicate soy-milk skin) pureed with *dashi* and soy sauce adds an elegant richness.

The first spoonful of this soup almost explodes on the palate with a vibrant, concentrated taste that is more intensely tomato-flavored than a fresh tomato could ever be.

中猪口 **July** *Naka-choko*

■ **Tomatoes** ■ *kumiage yuba*/**fresh soy-milk skin**
■ **roughly chopped cucumbers** ■ **chives** ■ *shiso* **buds**
recipe p.169

夏野菜煮合
Natsuyasai Takiawase

CHILLED SUMMER VEGETABLES

July's *hiyashi-bachi* is a healthy medley of six different Kyoto vegetables: eggplant, mild chili peppers, *gobo* (burdock) root, winter melon, pumpkin, and young lotus root. All these are common, and as everyone knows them so well, if I am going to serve them in my restaurant they will have to transcend their everyday image. I set about thinking about them in this way: in Kyoto, the adjective for something perfectly moist and soft is *minzuri*. When we think of nicely simmered eggplant, for example, we imagine it to be minzuri, soaked in dashi and bright navy blue. Similarly, well-simmered *togan* winter melon glistens like translucent jade. Pumpkin cooked in the same way should be more gently seasoned, lighter and softer and a little sweeter than the eggplant or winter melon. Minzuri young gobo root and young lotus root will be alabaster white and crisp in the mind's eye.

Sometimes it seems the more common and simple the dish is, the more difficult it is to prepare. These days, I strive to serve these kinds of dishes with confidence. I want to pass on the time-honored, classical methods behind them to future generations. I also would like young people to know the simple goodness of this traditional vegetable fare.

冷し鉢　July　*Hiyashi-bachi*

■ *Senryo nasu*/**Japanese eggplant** ■ *togan*/**winter melon** ■ **pumpkin**
■ **young lotus root** ■ **young** *gobo*/**burdock root**
■ **Tanaka chili peppers** ■ **green** *yuzu*　*recipe p.169*

豚角煮
Buta Kaku-ni

SIMMERED PORK CUBES

This hearty pork dish has been on our menu for generations, although my father's version was quite different from the one I serve today. It used to be called *natsugoshi no yakuseki*. "Natsugoshi" is the last day of June by the old calendar and "yakuseki" means medicine.

It was intended to be a tonic against the debilitating summer heat, since it was thought that the nourishing, calorie-rich meat would provide customers the necessary stamina to persevere. Previously the dish was given a fairly mild and sweet taste, but I've moved it in a more robust direction.

I simmer the pork all day in water that has been used to wash rice. This step removes most of the fat, but unfortunately it also removes a lot of flavor, so it then gets a brief simmer in a strong broth infused with *miso* and black sugar to boost the taste.

There is a Japanese saying: *"Aku wo motte, aku wo seisu,"* which means: "Defeat evil with evil." Here I've used its culinary equivalent by pitting the powerful, mineral-rich sweetness of black sugar against the harsh element of rustic *haccho* miso. This is one time I don't shy away from strong flavors.

蓋物 **July** *Futamono*

- **Pork belly** ■ **potato sauce** ■ **hot mustard** ■ **green beans**
- ■ *togan*/**winter melon** *recipe p.170*

生雲丹豆腐
Nama Uni-dofu

FRESH SEA URCHIN ROE TOFU

I love *uni* in July. It may be richer in August, but in July, fresh sea urchin roe is always sweet and truly redolent of its ocean home. This sea urchin tofu *sakizuke* is a cool invitation to the pleasures of summer. Tofu and uni share the same softness and density, so it seemed the marriage of the two would be a harmonious one. But it took nearly five years of trial and error to capture the meltingly ethereal texture I sought in this dish.

At first the soy milk and uni mixture refused to thicken with the addition of *nigari* magnesium salts, the traditional tofu maker's coagulant. So I added *kanten*, a seaweed gelatin, but the result was rubbery. Next I blended in some gelatin. This time the texture was hard and slippery. The silky consistency I'd been searching for was finally achieved by adjusting the ratio of soy milk to uni, and using nigari with just a dash of kanten and gelatin.

先付 **July** *Sakizuke*

■ **Soy milk** ■ **sea urchin roe** ■ *nigari*/**magnesium salts** ■ **gelatin**
■ *kanten*/**agar** *recipe p.170*

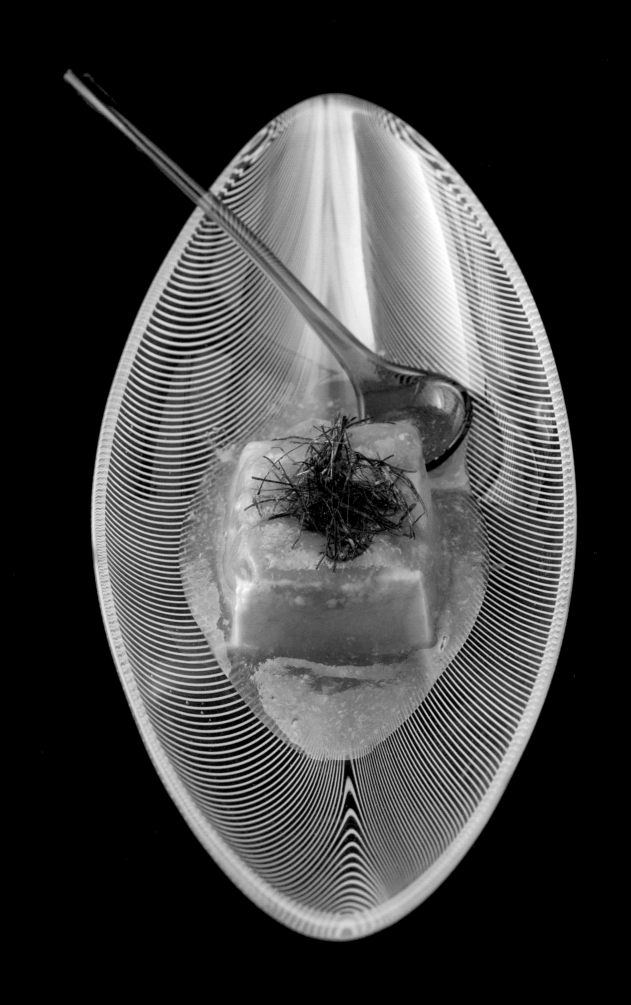

御造り

Otsukuri

Sashimi

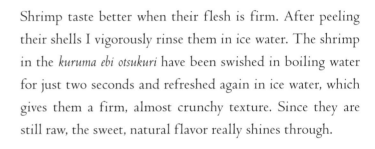

車海老　*Kuruma Ebi*

SHRIMP

Shrimp taste better when their flesh is firm. After peeling their shells I vigorously rinse them in ice water. The shrimp in the *kuruma ebi otsukuri* have been swished in boiling water for just two seconds and refreshed again in ice water, which gives them a firm, almost crunchy texture. Since they are still raw, the sweet, natural flavor really shines through.

縞鰺　*Shima Aji*

YELLOW JACK

Generally, fish that have a blue caste to their skin—such as *shima aji* yellow jack, *tsubasu* young yellowtail, *saba* mackerel and the like—have a thin, hard outer skin over a softer, silvery membrane. To make *sashimi*, we need to peel off the hard outer skin completely. Skillful chefs aim to remove it without blemishing the inner membrane, and to succeed at this demonstrates the freshness of the fish, since the meat must be very firm to allow it. Shima aji makes an especially good sashimi, its silver skin is iridescent, while the translucent flesh contrasts with an opaque strip of dark meat at the edge. Just one look will tell you how fresh it is.

向付　Summer *Mukozuke*

■ *Shima aji*/yellow jack ■ grated *wasabi* ■ Tosa soy sauce
■ *kuruma ebi*/shrimp ■ grated *wasabi*
■ Tosa soy sauce　*recipe p.170–171*

Hamo

PIKE CONGER

HAMO is a long eel-like fish that is often translated into English as pike eel or pike conger. It is such a part of summertime in Kyoto that the famed *Gion* Festival in July is often called the hamo festival. I have heard that the word "hamo" comes from *hamu*, meaning "bite" in Japanese. They certainly have a mouthful of razor-sharp teeth and a reputation for ferocity. Long ago, hamo caught in Osaka Bay were put into wooden buckets filled with water and delivered live to Kyoto by runners. The fact that the hamo arrived alive was an important consideration, as other kinds of fish were long dead by journey's end.

They say in the old days people only used hamo to flavor stock for *miso* soup because it was nearly impossible to remove the thousands of tiny bones in the fish. Eventually someone learned to make them palatable by shearing through the bones using a special heavy knife known as a *hamokiri bocho*. These eel-like fish have a beautiful white flesh and a refined taste. Even after improved transportation ushered in more variety at the fish markets, locals continue to adore hamo, Kyoto's toothsome taste of summer.

鱧落し
Hamo Otoshi

BLANCHED HAMO

The most important step in preparing *hamo* is the cutting of its myriad tiny bones. The bone-cutting knife is the biggest and heaviest knife I use. The hefty blade is more than a foot long and weighs over a pound. Like all traditional Japanese knives it is single edged like a chisel. Chefs often say hamo needs: "*Issun ni 24 hocho,*" which means 20 cuts to the inch (24 cuts to 3 centimeters)—a feat requiring a sharp knife and a sure hand. Just hearing the crunching rhythm of the knife as it clips through the bones makes me hungry.

The otoshi style is the simplest way to serve hamo, but this simplicity calls for much attention. I blanch sliced hamo fillets in boiling water and quickly plunge them into ice water to prevent them from overcooking. If they cook too long they can't be served.

Like cold *soba* noodles, hamo is best eaten immediately after it is prepared. In Kyoto, this dish is always served with an *ume* plum sauce, while in Osaka they eat it exclusively with *su*-miso, a vinegar and miso dressing. Residents of each city view their counterparts with pity, certain in the knowledge that theirs is the *only* way to enjoy hamo!

向付 **July *Mukozuke***

■ *Hamo* ■ *shiso* **buds** ■ *ume* **sauce**
■ **pickled melon as a serving dish** *recipe p.171*

鱧鍋
Hamo Nabe

HAMO HOT POT

A meal at Kikunoi includes about nine courses from the *saki-zuke* appetizer to rice—ten if you count *mizumono*. It is an *omakase* menu, meaning diners allow me to choose what they will eat. It's a responsibility I take seriously, and I always carefully consider the structure of the courses. The element of surprise is important, but if every plate is astonishing, the dining experience will lack balance; a meal requires something comforting and familiar too.

Hamo *nabe* (pot or stew) is one of these comforting dishes. It's an old fashioned creation based on Yanagawa nabe, a popular dish comprised of *dojo* loaches, *gobo* root and topped with beaten eggs. Sometimes sea eels or hamo are used in place of the dojo.

This nabe is a variation on the Yanagawa theme in which I combine hamo with roasted eggplant. The hamo is mild with a soft texture, while the eggplant is suffused with the hamo stock and exudes a slightly smoky aroma. I seal in the flavor at the end with a topping of beaten eggs. The dish offers customers something that's familiar, but definitely not the same old thing.

強肴 **August** *Shiizakana*

- *Hamo* ■ **eggplant** ■ **eggs** ■ *mitsuba*/**trefoil**
- *sansho*/**Japanese pepper powder**   *recipe p.171*

琥珀羹
Kohaku Kan

HAMO IN AMBER

The presentation of two jewel-like pieces of *hamo* jelly resting on a dew-moistened lotus leaf conjures a cool, watery image—an antidote to the sweltering heat of August. A lotus root garnish represents a *jyakago*, a kind of woven bamboo basket that is filled with stones and used to shore up riverbanks. Its presence adds another subtle aquatic touch. The amber jelly contains almost every part of the hamo including its meat, roe, liver and *hue*, the swim bladder.

I cook each part individually, and combine them in a rich hamo stock, which I set with gelatin. A single bite of the jelly is a microcosm of the fish itself. The bouquet of the dish also plays an important role. In Japanese cuisine, it was once taboo to combine different scents in one dish, but I think a medley of aromas can add complexity to a dish. In this case, I combine *shiso* buds, green *yuzu* citron, and ginger to evoke the fresh fragrance of summer.

先付 **August** *Sakizuke*

■ *Hamo* **meat, roe, liver and swim bladder** ■ **okra** ■ **lotus root**
■ **ginger juice** ■ *shiso* **buds** ■ **green** *yuzu*   *recipe p.171*

鮎塩焼き
Ayu Shio-yaki

GRILLED AYU

Ayu is a small but delicious freshwater fish that lives in rivers and feeds on aquatic plants. To select proper ayu, one must first choose a proper river. The ayu served at Kikunoi come from the Abo River, whose waters run cool and clear in its narrow banks until they drain into Lake Biwa.

I can see a certain savage nobility on the faces of the fish, which have navigated the Abo and eaten only wild mosses for their entire lives. I don't think they are worth eating unless they can be enjoyed straight from the stream. Taken fresh from the river, the small ayu (each weighs no more than an ounce/30 grams) are grilled over a charcoal fire. They cook slowly over the glowing coals until their skins are crisp. When cooked this way, they are edible from head to tail, including the bones.

Even the entrails are crunchy and aromatic, with a hint of bitterness that morphs into sweetness on the tongue. A liberal sprinkling of salt is needed to capture this fleeting bit of sweetness.

焼物 **June** *Yakimono*

■ *Ayu* ■ **tade-zu/water pepper vinegar** ■ *sudachi* *recipe p.171*

Awabi Iso-yaki

ABALONE IN A SALT DOME

When I came up with the *iso-yaki* baking method about twenty years ago, I was looking for a way to cook an abalone until tender without sacrificing its seashore aroma. I came up with the idea of wrapping the shellfish in *wakame* seaweed, covering it with salt and baking it in a big ceramic pot like pirates once used: a *horaku-nabe*. Because the heavy pot and salt made an almost airtight seal and retained heat, the abalone came out very tender and was still redolent of the ocean. The problem was, it took an hour to finish baking and the *horaku* pot took up a lot of space in the oven, making it difficult to serve this dish to a number of customers at the same time.

Nowadays, I steam the abalone until tender, then wrap it in *wakame*, top it with salt and bake it in a 320°F (160°C) oven for twenty minutes. I don't need the big pots any more, and the salt dome is nice and compact. When you remove the dome at your table, you can smell the fragrance of the tides. Then, gently pushing aside the wakame, you will discover a huge and meltingly soft abalone, stuffed with creamy sea urchin roe. Enjoy!

焼物 **August** *Yakimono*

■ **Abalone** ■ **fresh sea urchin roe** ■ **salted** *wakame*
■ *kimo dare*/**abalone liver sauce** ■ **salt dome**   *recipe p.172*

穴子飛龍頭
Anago Hirosu

SEA EEL TOFU BALLS

The fried tofu mixture called *hirosu* in the Kyoto dialect is known in standard Japanese as *gan-modoki*, meaning mock goose. It is a very homely and widely available food that customers know well, and dig into without trepidation.

Usually, hirosu is made from a mixture of tofu, grated *tsukune imo* (tsukune yam), chopped carrots, cloud ear mushrooms, ginkgo nuts and so forth, rolled into balls and deep-fried. They have a very soft texture and act like sponges to absorb the flavor of the liquid in which they are simmered. As delicious as they are, however, since Kikunoi is an elegant eatery, I am obliged to take these homely tofu balls to a higher level. To do this I combine tofu, grated tsukune yam, *kumiage yuba*, a little fresh cream, and toasted ground sesame seeds. Then I add the textural elements—carrots, cloud ear mushrooms and lily bulbs—and surround cooked sea eel with this mixture and deep-fry. After draining the excess oil I simmer them in lightly seasoned *dashi*. The fried tofu balls are already tender and rich, but what's more, the amino acid compounds in the sea eel and the dashi collaborate to intensify of the flavor. My goal here is to make something familiar, but surprisingly tastier than you might expect.

蓋物 **June** *Futamono*

- Tofu ■ *tsukune* yam ■ *kumiage yuba* ■ fresh cream
- toasted ground sesame seeds ■ carrots ■ cloud ear mushrooms
- lily bulbs ■ poppy seeds ■ *anago*/sea eel
- *kinome an*/leaf bud sauce ■ green peas
- *kinome*/Japanese pepper leaf buds *recipe p.172*

鱸雲丹焼き
Suzuki Uni-yaki

BROILED SEA BASS WITH SEA URCHIN ROE

This *suzuki* gets its crisp skin from a Chinese technique for cooking poultry. In Hong Kong I saw how boiling oil poured over a chicken could produce a parchment-crisp skin while leaving the meat tender and juicy. The same technique brings out the best in this favorite summer fish.

I begin the preparation by making cuts about a half-inch apart in sea bass fillets, taking care not to cut through the skin, then I skewer the filets and lightly flour the skin side. After ladling hot oil over the skin, I quickly broil the filets skin-side up over a charcoal fire. When the oil drips onto the hot coals it infuses the fish with a mild smokiness. Repeating the process two more times gives the skin a marvelous crunchiness, yet leaves the inside flesh tender and moist.

I finish the dish by filling the slices with fresh sea urchin roe and browning it under a salamander. The rich roe provides an ambrosial sauce. A sharp, green puree of *tade* (water pepper) and a tart squeeze of *sudachi* citrus provide an accent.

焼物 July *Yakimono*

- *Suzuki*/sea bass ■ uni/sea urchin roe
- *tade* puree/water pepper■ *sudachi*   *recipe p.172*

鴨ロース *Kamo Rosu*

ROAST DUCK BREAST

There are many ways to prepare *kamo rosu*, the roast duck breast that is a popular summer dish in Kyoto. My own method is first to sauté the breast, skin-side down, to brown it and remove excess fat from under the skin. Then I steam the duck in a soy sauce-based stock with a little sugar for six to seven minutes and then leave the duck and stock to cool separately. When the meat is cool, I put it back into the stock and steep it well. In Western cuisine, I imagine chefs cook the duck without wasting a single drop of blood, but I remove it. I want the meat to be rare, but I don't wish to serve something dripping blood. The sliced breast has a beautiful rosy color and a subtle but meaty flavor. You don't need a sauce to enjoy this dish, but if you like, a dab of Dijon mustard will suit.

冷し鉢 June *Hiyashi-bachi*

- Duck breast ■ white *zuiki*/taro stems ■ snow peas
- Dijon mustard   *recipe p.172*

Tsukemono-zushi

PICKLE SUSHI

The oppressive heat and humidity of Kyoto's rainy season is enough to stifle anyone's urge to eat. When the thought of a heavy meal is too much to bear, I always look for a simple, refreshing dish to restore my flagging appetite. Something like pickles made of *mizu-nasu* and *myoga* ginger flower buds on sushi rice is always welcome. It's light, clean tasting and sits ever so gently on the stomach. Mizu-nasu is an especially tender and delicious eggplant that is cultivated only in Osaka; I like to pickle it in rice bran, a traditional method called *dobo-zuke* in the Kyoto dialect.

It takes a lot of effort to make a good dobo-zuke. The rice-bran pickling medium needs daily tending and each vegetable requires a precise amount of time in the mixture to ripen fully. Lately folks can't be bothered to pickle vegetables at home, so my customers are delighted to find a good dobo-zuke made with only rice bran, salt and vegetables. This is one traditional food I would hate to see fade away.

御飯 **June** *Gohan*

- *Dobo-zuke mizu-nasu*/**rice-bran pickled egg plant** ▪ **sushi rice**
- *myoga*/**ginger blossom pickles** ▪ *hajikami*/**pickled ginger shoots**
recipe p.173

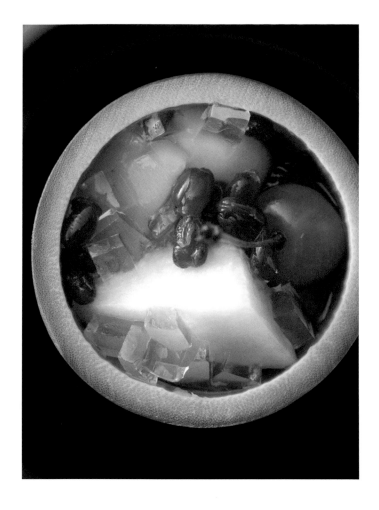

夏の水物 *Natsu no Mizumono*

SUMMER MIZUMONO

In summer, I make a number of changes at Kikunoi to try to beat the stifling heat. For better ventilation, I replace the *shoji* paper screens with *yoshizu* straw screens; I also cover the *tatami* mats with *ajiro* wicker mats, which are cooler to the touch. We burn a lighter style of incense, made of fragrant sandalwood, and the waitresses slip into cooler kimonos of silk gauze. Though I have air conditioners in the dining rooms, I doubt they could ever replace a gentle, natural breeze.

Summer calls for cooling sweets too, so at the main restaurant I serve two popular old-time desserts: *mitsu-mame*; beans and *kanten* with syrup, and *uji-kintoki*; shaved ice with green tea syrup and sweet red bean paste. A feeling of nostalgia comes easily when relaxing on the tatami after a big meal on a quiet summer's eve. The faces of young and old alike take on a dreamy aspect as talk turns to the old days. Traditional sweets are the perfect accompaniment for these precious summer moments.

蜜豆 *Mitsu-mame*
MIXED SWEETS IN SYRUP
■ *Kanten*/seaweed gelatin ■ simmered red beans
■ *shiratama*/rice-flour dumplings ■ cherries ■ melon ■ mango
■ sugar syrup *recipe p.173*

宇治金時 *Uji-kintoki*
SHAVED ICE WITH GREEN TEA SYRUP
■ Shaved ice ■ green tea powder ■ sugar syrup
■ *shiratama*/rice-flour dumplings ■ sweet red bean paste
recipe p.173

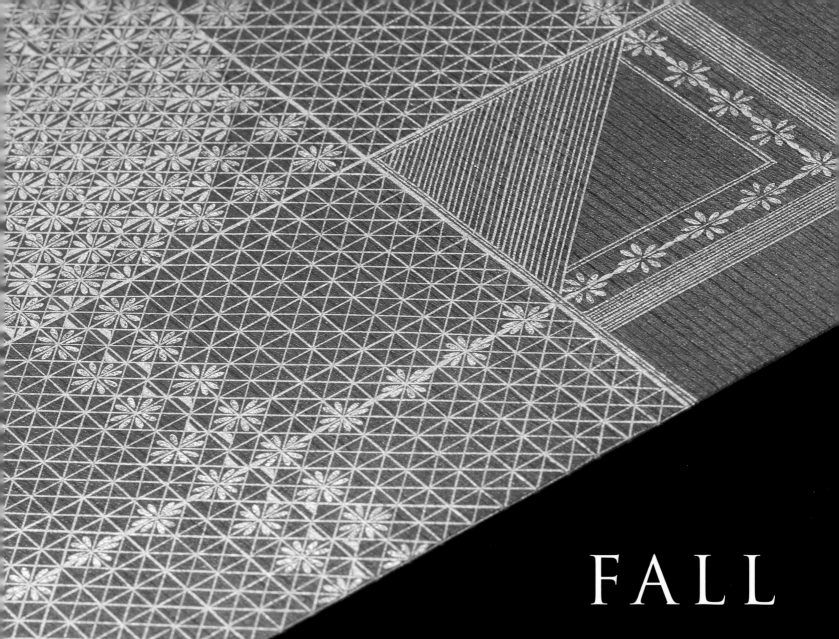

FALL

長月の八寸 *Nagatsuki no Hassun*

SEPTEMBER HASSUN

September is the month for *otsukimi*; full-moon watching. I personally think this month is a good time to enjoy all phases of the moon, not just its full stage. In Kyoto, we pay homage to the moon by making dumplings shaped like a small taro and covered in sweet red-bean paste. Unfortunately from Kikunoi we cannot actually see the moon, so I hang a scroll painting of it. In this month's *hassun* I want to evoke a feeling of watching the moon from a boat on a lake. The moon is reflected on the surface of the water upon which autumn leaves are floating. When you look to the shore, you can see stalks of *susuki* pampas grass waving silently in the moonlight.

鯛菊花寿司 *Tai Kikka-zushi*
SEA BREAM CHRYSANTHEMUM SUSHI
Chrysanthemum shaped sushi made of sushi rice flecked with chrysanthemum flowers and *yuzu*, topped with vinegared sea bream

鱧八幡巻き *Hamo Hachiman-maki*
HAMO AND GOBO ROLL
Simmered *gobo* root wrapped in *hamo*

海老松風 *Ebi Matsukaze*
SHRIMP CAKE
Baked loaf made of shrimp, fish paste and egg, sprinkled with white poppy seeds

焼き目栗茶巾 *Yakime Kuri Chakin*
WRAPPED CHESTNUT
Pureed chestnuts shaped into a ball using a moist towel, baked in the oven until golden brown

銀杏芋 *Icho Imo*
GINKGO SWEET POTATO
Sweet potato punched into ginkgo leaf shapes and deep-fried

ガラサ海老老酒漬けのすだち釜・鱒の子
Garasa Ebi Laochu-zuke no Sudachi-gama/Masu no Ko
GRASS SHRIMP IN SHAOXING RICE WINE WITH TROUT ROE
Grass shrimp are small translucent shrimp. I shell them live and soak in Shaoxing rice wine, then fill a *sudachi* cup with them and top with salted trout roe.

塩粉吹き銀杏 *Shio Kofuki Ginnan*
SALTED GINKGO NUTS
Ginkgo nuts toasted with sake and salt

松葉素麺 *Matsuba Somen*
GREEN TEA NOODLE FANS
Fans of thin noodles, deep-fried to resemble pine needle sprays *recipes p.174*

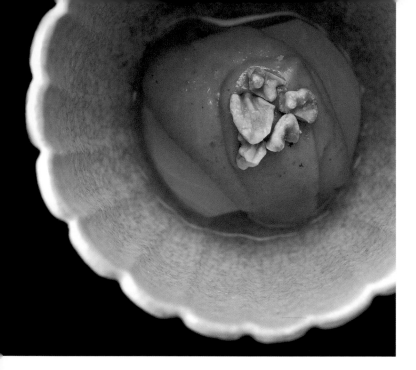

蕪風呂吹き
Kabura Furofuki

TURNIPS WITH MISO SAUCE

October is the month when small white turnips known as *ko-kabura* are coming into season. In Kyoto these turnips are traditionally paired with a *yuzu*-flavored *miso* paste—delicious, but not very creative cooking. Walnuts are quite autumnal, so I've combined some with sesame seeds and miso to make a sauce that gives the root vegetables a little glamor. A sprinkling of chopped walnuts adds a crunchy counterpoint to the soft texture of the miso and turnips. A final garnish of yellow yuzu julienne is a bow to tradition and adds a sassy fragrance.

To prepare the turnips, peel them, put them in a saucepan with cold water and a piece of *kombu*, and slowly bring to a boil. Pay attention to the cooking time because turnips are not as sturdy as *daikon*, and can easily turn to mush if overcooked. When a bamboo skewer easily pierces them, remove the kombu and drain half the cooking liquid, then add dried bonito flakes, *dashi*, light soy sauce, *mirin* and salt to taste. Let the turnips cool in the stock. This last step gives the dish a more well-rounded flavor.

先付 October *Sakizuke*

■ *Ko-kabura*/small turnips ■ **walnuts** ■ **white sesame seeds**
■ *Saikyo miso* **paste** ■ **yellow** *yuzu* recipe p.174

胡桃豆腐
Kurumi-dofu

WALNUT TOFU

The *sakizuke* course that welcomes customers to Kikunoi is finished in a couple of smooth spoonfuls. This important first impression should be refined, but neither too demanding to eat, nor too filling.

September's walnut-based sakizuke meets these criteria. At first glance it appears simple, but after a nibble you'll notice there is a complex interplay between its pudding-like smoothness, the tannic mouth-feel, and crunchy texture of the nuts.

To make this dish, I combine toasted ground walnuts, ground white sesame seeds and *Kumagawa hon-kuzu* with *dashi*. After straining the mixture I simmer it for about twenty minutes, stirring continuously as it thickens. To this base I add coarsely chopped toasted walnuts and oil, and let it firm up in the refrigerator.

The combination of chopped and ground nuts and oil conveys the full range of tastes and textures of the walnut. Ripe Delaware grapes and a sprinkling of *wasabi* jelly contribute a juicy yet piquant finishing touch.

先付 September *Sakizuke*

■ **Walnuts** ■ **white sesame seeds** ■ *Kumagawa hon-kuzu/kuzu* **starch**
■ **Delaware grapes** ■ *hanaho jiso/shiso* **buds** ■ *wasabi* **jelly**
recipe p.175

豊年椀
Honen-wan

HARVEST SOUP

This bountiful soup is my celebration of the autumn harvest. Its main ingredient is that ubiquitous Kyoto fish, the *hamo*. The inspiration for this dish is a toasted rice soup normally found in *cha-kaiseki* called *yuto*, made by salvaging the rice that sticks to the bottom of the cooking pot, and simmering it in plenty of water. I was looking to capture its toasty aroma and palate-cleansing simplicity in my soup.

I also added some *matsutake* mushrooms to amplify the scent of the toasted rice. The hamo is crusted with toasted rice, deep fried and simmered in broth to represent a traditional straw rice bag known as a *kome dawara*.

To serve, I decorate a bowl with warmed egg tofu, *mibuna* greens, matsutake mushrooms and the fried hamo. Then I pour hot broth on top and garnish with *yuzu* peel.

蓋物　September *Nimono-wan*

■ **Toasted rice** ■ *hamo* ■ *matsutake* **mushrooms**
■ **egg tofu** ■ *mibuna*/**mustard greens** ■ *yuzu*　*recipe p.175*

雲子銀餡蒸し
Kumoko Gin-an-mushi

STEAMED COD ROE WITH SILVER SAUCE

This dish arrives at the table in a covered cup no bigger than a demitasse. When diners whisk off the lid and look inside they find piping-hot cod roe—*kumoko*—lapped with *gin-an*—silver sauce. The roe is luscious and melts away like cream while the thick dashi is soothing. Almost too soon the contents of the cup have vanished, leaving only a clean aftertaste of ginger.

When the serving size is just right, the customer is left yearning for yet another spoonful. That's the way it should be, as this *sakizuke* is meant to warm people on a chilly autumn eve and put them at ease, not fill them up. I'm always happy when diners begin eating with a sense of anticipation of good things to come.

先付　November *Sakizuke*

■ *Kumoko*/**cod roe** ■ *gin-an*/**silver sauce** ■ **ginger**
■ **chopped chives**　*recipe p.175*

神無月の八寸 *Kaminazuki no Hassun*

OCTOBER HASSUN

October is the end of the year by the tea ceremony calendar and is when the last of the previous year's tea must be used; by November the spring-harvested leaves will be ready. Autumn is now further along and the crickets that were once heard chirping enthusiastically are becoming scarce. Soon, even these hardy few will be gone. With October's *hassun* course, I want to evoke a little of the sad and sentimental feeling we have for these departing friends.

On a round tray, I place a small cricket cage, a leaf of *kuzu* arrowroot—one of seven autumn flowers, and a flower of *hagi*—a Japanese bush clover. The cricket cage is filled with fall delicacies and customers can take a close look at each one as they carefully remove the cage without disturbing the display.

かます焼き目寿司 *Kamasu Yakime-zushi*
BARRACUDA SUSHI

A stick of vinegared barracuda sushi. Before serving, I singe the skin quickly for a crisp texture and toasty aroma, then garnish with *sudachi*.

鮎白子と真子うるかのすだち釜・鱒の子
Ayu Shirako to Mako Uruka no Sudachi-gama/Masu no Ko
SALTED AYU ENTRAILS WITH TROUT ROE

Uruka is salted ayu entrails. *Mako uruka* is made from the fish's ovaries and *shirako uruka* from the milt. I combine them in a *sudachi* cup before topping with salted trout roe.

焼き目栗 *Yakime Guri*
GRILLED CHESTNUTS

Grilled chestnuts simmered in sweetened syrup

鱧の子落雁 *Hamo no Ko Rakugan*
HAMO ROE MOUSSE

Steamed *hamo* roe simmered in dashi and combined with fish paste and egg

銀杏芋 *Icho Imo*
GINKGO SWEET POTATO

As served in September

翡翠銀杏 *Hisui Ginnan*
JADE GINKGO NUTS

Jade green ginkgo nuts toasted with sake and salt

松葉素麺 *Matsuba Somen*
GREEN TEA NOODLE FANS

As served in September *recipes p.175*

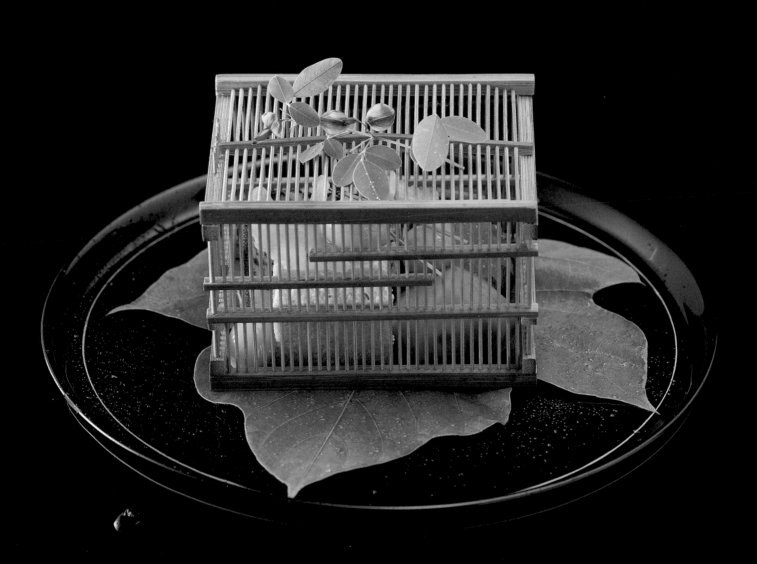

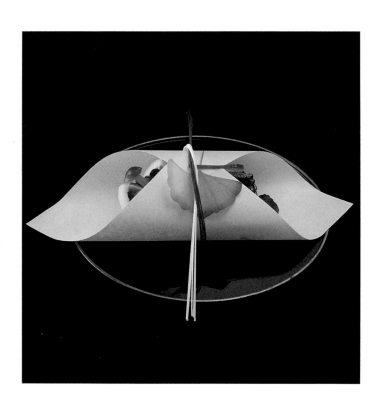

霜月の八寸 *Shimotsuki no Hassun*

NOVEMBER HASSUN

November is the month of the Gencho festival, which origi-
nated as a royal ritual in the Heian Era. On the first day
of the tenth month of the lunar calendar (*I no tsuki*, the
Month of the Boar), the emperor made rice cakes, ate them
and prayed for sound health. These days, *I no ko mochi*—a
sweet rice dumpling covered in red bean or sesame paste
shaped into a wild boar—is eaten. Originally, the cakes were
wrapped in paper and tied with red and white string. This
inspired me to wrap the *hassun* in paper.

割山椒柚子釜盛り *Wari-zansho Yuzu-gama Mori*
YUZU SANSHO CUP

I hollow out a *yuzu* citrus into the shape of a *wari-zansho*—a split Japanese
peppercorn—and fill it with monkfish liver, *mibuna* greens, and seasoned
shimeji mushrooms.

紅葉烏賊 *Momiji Ika*
AUTUMN LEAVES SQUID

Squid that is broiled, smeared with salted sea urchin roe then punched
into the shape of a maple leaf

からすみ *Karasumi*
CURED MULLET ROE

Sliced cured mullet roe that becomes available in autumn

昆布籠 *Kombu Kago*
KOMBU BASKET

Edible basket woven from thinly sliced *kombu* kelp

鴨肝松風 *Kamo Kimo Matsukaze*
DUCK LIVER TERRINE

Miso-flavored terrine of duck liver, pine nuts, and brandied raisins

慈姑煎餅 *Kuwai Senbei*
WATER CHESTNUT CRACKERS (NOT PICTURED)

Deep-fried thinly sliced water chestnuts, sprinkled with salt

栗煎餅 *Kuri Senbei*
CHESTNUT CRACKERS (NOT PICTURED)

Deep-fried chestnut slices, sprinkled with salt

塩粉吹き銀杏 *Shio Kofuki Ginnan*
SALTED GINKGO NUTS

As served in September

松葉素麺 *Matsuba Somen*
GREEN TEA NOODLE FANS

As served in September *recipes p.176*

御造り
Otsukuri

Sashimi

つばす
Tsubasu

YOUNG YELLOWTAIL

Yellowtail are what we call *shusse uo*—fish that are known by different names as they develop. A very young yellowtail is a *tsubasu*; a little bigger and it becomes *hamachi*; bigger still is *mejiro* and finally, when fully grown, it is a *buri*. Confusing? Well, those names are just for Kansai western Japan; in the eastern region of Kanto, at equivalent stages the fish are: *wakashi*, *inada*, *warasa* and buri. As far as we can tell, our ancestors who named them just didn't think a tsubasu, which is only ten inches long, and a *buri* at over three feet, were the same fish.

Indeed, they differ not only in size, but in taste. While the appeal of the tsubasu is its austere delicacy, the taste of *buri* is buttery, rich, and powerful. From September to October, fishermen catch tsubasu as they migrate from Japan's Inland Sea to the Pacific Ocean. Their flesh is smooth, translucent and tinged a light pink. The taste is extremely delicate—sweet and not at all oily. Soy sauce would overwhelm it, so if you want to savor the tsubasu's subtlety, the only garnish you need is a pinch of good sea salt and a few drops of tart *sudachi* juice.

向付 **Fall *Mukozuke***

■ *Tsubasu*/young yellowtail ■ salt ■ sudachi
recipe p.177

鯖 *Saba*

MACKEREL

We Kyoto-ites adore mackerel. While we love white-fleshed fish, especially sea bream, we love mackerel as well. And guests from other countries seem to share our enthusiasm. Though I imagine a first encounter with this dark blue fish could be daunting, whenever I serve it to foreign guests, after one bite they always say: "Wow! This is fantastic!" Chefs among them often ask how to make *shime saba* pickled mackerel.

The mackerel I use weigh about two pounds each and are line-caught in the Inland Sea. They are extremely fresh—the meat is very dense and rich. As it's the best mackerel you can get in Japan, it is good enough to eat raw, yet in Kyoto we

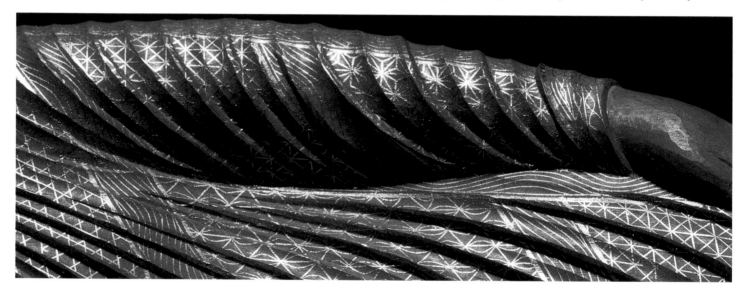

prefer it lightly pickled with vinegar. The good thing about pickled mackerel is that the salt and vinegar remove excess water and fishy odors, and concentrate the flavor. But care must be taken—if the vinegar is too strong or you soak the fish for too long, the meat dries out. Since the flesh is very tender, I like to slice it into thick pieces. Yet the skin can be a little tough, so I make cuts through it. I think *pon-zu* and grated ginger make a splendid accompaniment. Mackerel tastes just marvelous when the *pon-zu* soaks into the slices.

向付 **Fall *Mukozuke***

■ *Shime saba*/**pickled mackerel** ■ *pon-zu* ■ **grated ginger**
recipe p.177

松茸土瓶蒸し
Matsutake Dobin-mushi

STEAMED MATSUTAKE TEAPOT

Every culture has certain irresistible aromas that waft from its kitchens. The yeasty smell of freshly baked bread or a garlicky spaghetti sauce simmering on the stove are two that come to mind. Without a doubt, the favorite culinary fragrance in Japan is *kobashii*. It is the smell of something toasted, even scorched a little.

Maybe it speaks to our ancestral memory of grains roasting over an open hearth, but for whatever reason, when that kobashii scent hits my nose, it never fails to make my mouth water. This proclivity for toasty aromas may account for our love affair with the *matsutake* mushroom, which smells quite like roasting grain when grilled.

October's *futamono* matches this sought-after mushroom with *hamo* in a soup. The serving vessel is a small ceramic teapot. The lid of the pot is a small cup. When you pour the soup into the cup, the rich aroma that was sealed inside the pot gently reveals itself and the flavor of the broth unfurls. Though flavorful, the hamo does not overwhelm the matsutake. Some people season the broth by squeezing *sudachi* juice into the pot itself, but I think this is overkill. If the flavor needs refreshing, a few drops in the cup should suffice.

蓋物 October *Futamono*

■ *Matsutake* mushrooms ■ *hamo* ■ *mitsuba*/trefoil ■ *sudachi*
recipe p.177

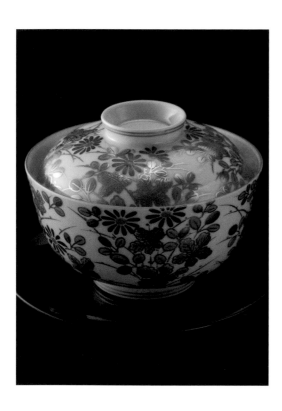

若狭ぐじ粟蒸し
Wakasa Guji Awa-mushi

TILEFISH STEAMED WITH MILLET

November is an important month for those who follow *sado*, the way of tea. The re-opening of the hearth in a ritual known as *robiraki* ushers in a new year of tea. The cast-iron teapot is returned to its place on the hearth and the first of the Spring-harvested tea is used in a ceremony called *kuchi-kiri chaji*. I welcome the event with steamed tilefish and millet, garnished auspiciously with red carrots and white *daikon*.

Millet was once an important grain in the Japanese diet, but is rarely eaten these days. I had wanted to use it to coat an ingredient for soup. Unfortunately, millet lacks the necessary stickiness and my first attempts ended in failure. But I didn't give up, and finally succeeded by mixing the grain with a little *domyoji*, a kind of glutinous rice powder.

When I combine the two with lightly seasoned dashi and steam it, the mixture comes out soft like a *mochi* rice cake. I use it to cover *shiitake* mushrooms and chestnuts, which I then wrap in a piece of Wakasa tilefish. This dish offers a visual feast as well, with the contrasting colors of its green chrysanthemum sauce, white daikon and red carrots.

蓋物 November *Futamono*

■ *Awa* **millet** ■ *domyoji* ■ **Wakasa tilefish** ■ **chestnuts**
■ *shiitake* **mushrooms** ■ **chrysanthemum leaves** ■ *daikon*
■ **red carrot** ■ *yuzu* *recipe p.177*

かます杉板焼き
Kamasu Sugiita-yaki

PLANKED BARRACUDA

In October when *kamasu* barracuda have fattened nicely, I cure them in *Yuanji*, a marinade comprised of soy sauce, *mirin*, *miso and* sake. When the fish fillets have soaked up the flavor, I top them with some *shiitake* mushrooms and sandwich them between two thin planks of cedar that have been soaked in water. After binding the wooden packets with a bamboo string, I bake them at 350°F/190°C for fifteen minutes. The soft scent of cedar suffuses the gently baked fillets and they are fabulous. The presentation of this dish is something of a grand spectacle as well. The thin cedar planks come out of the oven dry but not burned. I singe them with a propane torch to set them alight and arrange them on a large platter covered in autumn leaves for the servers to carry into the dining room. The sight of the smoldering cedar planks and the scent of their smoky incense put one in a reflective mood and stir a nostalgic longing for the hearth.

焼物　October *Yakimono*

■ *Kamasu*/barracuda ■ *shiitake* mushrooms ■ *mukago* (see glossary)
■ *sudachi* ■ *miso yuanji*/*miso* marinade　recipe p.177

子持ち鮎
Komochi Ayu

AYU WITH ROE

In May, June and July, the best way to enjoy *ayu* is simply to eat it salted and crisply grilled over charcoal. In August, too, there is much enjoyment to be found in a bowl of *ayu meshi*, ayu cooked with rice. Finally, September ushers in a delicious close to the ayu season with roe-filled *komochi* ayu.

As summer ends, the fish's belly swells with roe and its skin becomes tougher. I like to slowly broil it over charcoal; as it cooks, the skin tightens and the roe expands. At that point it already looks good enough to eat, but I patiently keep broiling them until the skin is good and crisp. Real fish aficionados appreciate the tempting smell of a little edge of burned skin.

When it is cooked I remove the backbone and serve the last ayu of the season with sweetened walnuts, whose tannins cut the richness of the fish. I serve it atop a round plate—an allusion to the autumn moon, which itself reflects the roundness of the plump komochi ayu.

焼物 September *Yakimono*

■ *Ayu* with roe ■ walnuts *recipe p.178*

鴨朴葉焼き
Kamo Hoba-yaki

DUCK GRILLED ON
A MAGNOLIA LEAF

Hoba-yaki is a rustic way of cooking duck on a *miso*-filled magnolia leaf, which always conjures a vision of hunters warming themselves around a fire in a mountain hut. The dish would lose its meaning if I fussed with it too much, so I just let customers cook it themselves at the table on a wonderful ceramic barbecue called a *shichirin*. It is a really simple preparation, but tastes out of this world with a sip of sake.

Without changing the original simplicity of the dish, I use miso that has been cooked with sake to tone down its saltiness and add egg yolks and sesame seeds for a rich glossy texture. The finely sliced leeks on top are an absolute must with duck, and a little grated *yuzu* zest helps bring out the aroma of the miso.

焼物 November *Yakimono*

■ *Miso* paste ■ duck breast ■ chestnuts ■ *ginnan*/ginkgo nuts
■ *hari negi*/finely sliced white leeks ■ *yuzu*
recipe p.178

柿なます
Kaki Namasu

JAPANESE PERSIMMON NAMASU

November is a month when root vegetables are in season. One of the best from the Kyoto region is *Kintoki ninjin*, a vivid red carrot that has quite a strong taste compared to its Western counterpart. *Daikon* is getting sweeter this month too. To make this palate-cleansing vinegared dish, or *suno-mono*, I first cut the carrot and daikon into rectangular slices and lightly sprinkle with salt. After wringing them dry, I add sliced persimmon and sprinkle the mixture with a mild vinegar called *Tosa-zu*, which is seasoned with soy sauce and bonito flakes. *Mitsuba*, a pungent green herb, lends a dash of color and *yuzu* is added for fragrance.

I like my customers to eat a lot; my father disapproved of this, but I can't help it—I want them to enjoy all kinds of delicious things. The sunomono acts as a little break that perks up the taste buds so the diners can enjoy whatever else I have in store for them.

酢肴 November *Su-zakana*

- *Kaki*/Japanese persimmons ■ *kintoki ninjin*/red carrots
- *daikon*/giant radishes ■ *mitsuba*/trefoil
- *hari yuzu*/finely sliced yuzu skin ■ *Tosa-zu*

recipe p.178

焼き茄子と鰊煮合
Yakinasu to Nishin Takiawase

GRILLED JAPANESE EGGPLANT AND SIMMERED HERRING

This hearty dish is based on *obanzai* cooking; the everyday food of the common folk in Kyoto. *Migaki nishin*, a dried herring from northern Japan, has long been an obanzai staple. Like salt cod in Europe, the inexpensive dried herring was an important source of protein for Kyoto-ites faced with a paucity of fresh fish.

In their dried state the herrings are quite salty and bitter, requiring no small effort to make them palatable. First they need a couple of days' soaking in the milky water left over from washing rice. Then, this Japanese version of "slow food" needs to be cooked for two days to tone down its strong fishy smell. Migaki herring really needs to be paired with another assertive ingredient. Autumn-harvested Japanese eggplant is a good match. Summer eggplant is fresh and juicy, but in autumn it is both richer and bitter tasting at the same time. This bitterness suits the herring well.

All over the world, regional cuisines have evolved when cooks use ingredients at hand to create dishes that fit the local climate and lifestyle. These local cuisines have at their heart a basic honesty and integrity that modern chefs would do well to emulate.

煮合 September *Takiawase*

■ *Migaki nishin* ■ Japanese eggplant
■ *shungiku*/chrysanthemum leaves ■ *yuzu*
recipe p.178

金鍔伊勢海老白味噌仕立て
Kin-tsuba Ise Ebi Shiro-miso-jitate

GOLDEN SPINY LOBSTER WITH WHITE MISO

I like to think of this dish as a *tour de force* of *Ise ebi* (as the spiny lobster is called in Japan). Its success rests on three important elements: first there is the *shiro-miso-jitate*, a lobster-based soup finished with white miso. I put lobster bodies, including the flavorful tomalley, and shells in a pan, pour a substantial amount of sake over them and cook over high heat. This removes any fishy smells and provides a rich lobster stock. After straining the stock and adding *dashi*, I finish the soup with white miso paste. This soup is a Japanese take on the French bisque, a creamy soup made with lobsters or other shellfish. Instead of cream, my version relies on white miso paste to soften the sharp taste of the lobster.

The second element involves coating the lobster meat with egg yolks and quickly deep-frying until it is just rare. After a quick dousing with boiling water to remove excess oil, the fried lobster pieces are lightly simmered in the miso stock. I like to serve the lobster meat about medium done, when its succulent sweetness is strongest.

The third aspect of this dish is the garnish. Since the soup is rich and the lobster is so full-bodied, it begs for a simple element to give the taste buds a little break. A garnish of lightly boiled turnips and their greens works deliciously.

強肴 November *Shiizakana*

■ *Ise ebi*/spiny lobster ■ Shogoin turnips ■ white *miso* paste
■ egg yolks ■ yellow *yuzu*
recipe p.178

干し海鼠子 マスカット糀漬け
Hoshi Konoko Muscat Koji-zuke

DRIED KONOKO WITH KOJI-PICKLED MUSCAT GRAPES

Konoko is the roe of the sea cucumber. Harvested in spring, it is processed and dried in the sun and wind until autumn, when the dried roe, called *hoshi konoko*, is ready to eat. It comes in a variety of shapes; one favorite style is called *bachiko*, which resembles a triangular *shamisen* plectrum. This marvelous delicacy tastes like the concentrated essence of the seashore. Its rich flavor and fragrance should be savored with a fine sake, Champagne, or a good Riesling.

My father created the original recipe for *koji* pickled Muscat grapes, which was very trendy at the time. I've changed the recipe a bit, but I still enjoy the fruity perfume of the Muscat grapes, the sweetness of the koji, and the sharpness of Japanese mustard.

The combination of pickled grapes and the dried sea cucumber roe brings out the best in each ingredient and makes the accompanying sake or wine tantalizingly more-ish.

中猪口 September *Naka-choko*

- Dried *konoko* ■ muscat grapes ■ *koji* (see glossary)
- Japanese mustard

recipe p.179

Hamo Matsu Don

HAMO AND MATSUTAKE MUSHROOM RICE BOWL

My *matsu don* is a study in luxurious simplicity. I bring seasoned *dashi* and chopped *hamo* to a boil, add a substantial heap of thickly sliced *matsutake* mushrooms, and cook quickly. I cover it all with beaten eggs to seal in the flavor and, just before the eggs are set, I sprinkle the dish with *mitsuba* and serve over hot steamed rice. Chemistry also comes into play, with the mutually flavor-enhancing effects of the inosinic acid in the hamo reacting with the guanylic acid in the matsutake.

Customers are often taken aback by the profusion of costly mushrooms in the dish. Some might think it extravagant, but I want diners to truly experience the matsutake's meaty texture and sylvan aroma. If I were constrained to using only a few stingy slivers of matsutake in this recipe, then I'd rather make an honest *oyako don* (chicken and egg bowl). As long as I'm cooking, I'll be salting the food the way I like and using the ingredients in any way that satisfies my culinary goals.

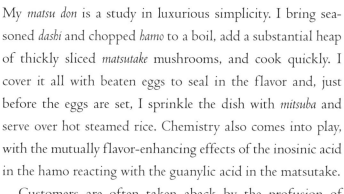

御飯 October *Gohan*

■ *Matsutake* **mushrooms** ■ **eggs** ■ *hamo* **fillets**
■ *mitsuba*/**trefoil** ■ *sansho*/**Japanese pepper**
recipe p.179

FALL MIZUMONO

I can't count how many ice cream recipes I have collected. We make sorbet and custard puddings as well, but once I decide to create a certain kind of ice cream, I don't give up until its flavor, texture and every other aspect is exactly as I imagined. I try to combine ice cream or sorbet with something that softens its cold impact on the mouth. For example, I serve sorbet made of *kabosu*—a refreshingly tart, lime-like citrus—with *ichijiku-kan* (fig jelly), and *ogura-kan* (red bean jelly). I add cinnamon to the fig jelly and put some grated ginger and lemon juice in the red bean jelly. These sweets are an interesting hybrid of Eastern and Western tastes.

Another hybrid dessert is *hoji-cha* (roasted tea) ice cream with *Tanba-ji matsukaze* (black soybean bean cake). Roasted tea ice cream has a provocative, toasty fragrance and a refreshing aftertaste. As for the cake, I intended to bake it using only Tanba black soybeans, but added more ingredients that can be found between Kyoto and Tanba—such as autumn fruits and nuts—and it evolved into this original gateau.

かぼすソルベ *Kabosu Sorbet*
KABOSU SORBET
■ *Kabosu* citrus ■ sugar   *recipe p.179*

無花果羹 *Ichijiku-kan*
FIG JELLY
■ *Ichijiku*/figs ■ sugar ■ cinnamon ■ pearl agar   *recipe p.179*

小豆羹 *Azuki-kan*
RED BEAN JELLY
■ Red bean paste ■ lemon juice ■ lemon zest
■ grated ginger ■ gelatin   *recipe p.179*

焙じ茶アイスクリーム *Hoji-cha Ice Cream*
ROASTED TEA ICE CREAM
■ *Hoji-cha*/roasted tea ■ milk ■ egg yolks ■ granulated sugar
recipe p.179

丹波路松風 *Tanba-ji Matsukaze*
BLACK SOYBEAN CAKE
■ Black soybeans simmered with sugar ■ peeled chestnuts
■ pine nuts ■ raisins ■ dried figs ■ poppy seeds ■ yuzu ■ pastry flour
■ baking powder ■ butter ■ eggs ■ milk ■ honey ■ granulated sugar
recipe p.179

WINTER

DECEMBER HASSUN

December's *hassun* is inspired by my childhood memory of camellias glimpsed through a fence. On my way to school, there was a place where delicate pink *sazanka* (*Camellia sasanqua*) flowers could be seen behind a bamboo trellis. Even as a mischievous schoolboy, I was stopped in my tracks by their beauty. My life has taken many turns since then, but I clearly remember that scene, and I hope that this hassun will stir a few fond memories in my customers too.

The original partitioned plate was made by Rosanjin Kitaoji, one the greatest masters of twentieth-century ceramics. It imitates the compartments of a palette used for Japanese-style painting. With its lid in place, it resembles an ink-stone case and you have no idea what might be inside. When the top comes off, the delicious contents are spectacularly revealed.

椿寿司 *Tsubaki-zushi*
CAMELLIA SUSHI
Smoked salmon sushi in the shape of a camellia

小川からすみ *Ogawa Karasumi*
DRIED MULLET ROE ROLLED WITH SQUID
Dried mullet roe is wrapped in a layer of raw squid
then pickled in sake lees.

助子 *Sukeko*
COD ROE
The cod roe is simmered in lightly seasoned dashi. I let the roe cool
in the stock, to absorb its mild flavor.

菜の花芥子和え *Nanohana Karashi-ae*
RAPINI WITH JAPANESE MUSTARD DRESSING
The rapini is quickly blanched and then soaked in dashi seasoned with soy
sauce. Finally I dress it with Japanese mustard.

海鼠小角蕪みぞれ和え *Namako Kokaku Kabu Mizore-ae*
SEA CUCUMBER AND TURNIPS
After tenderizing fresh sea cucumber in boiling *ban-cha* tea, I cut it into
bite-size pieces and soak in *Tosa-zu* vinegar. Then I mix it with diced turnips
and grated daikon radish. Finely diced yuzu skin provides a fragrant garnish.

芥子蓮根 *Karashi Renkon*
FRIED LOTUS ROOT WITH JAPANESE MUSTARD
I stuff the holes of lotus roots with a mixture of white miso paste,
minced meat, and Japanese mustard, coat with dried bonito flakes,
then deep-fry and slice before serving. *recipes p.180*

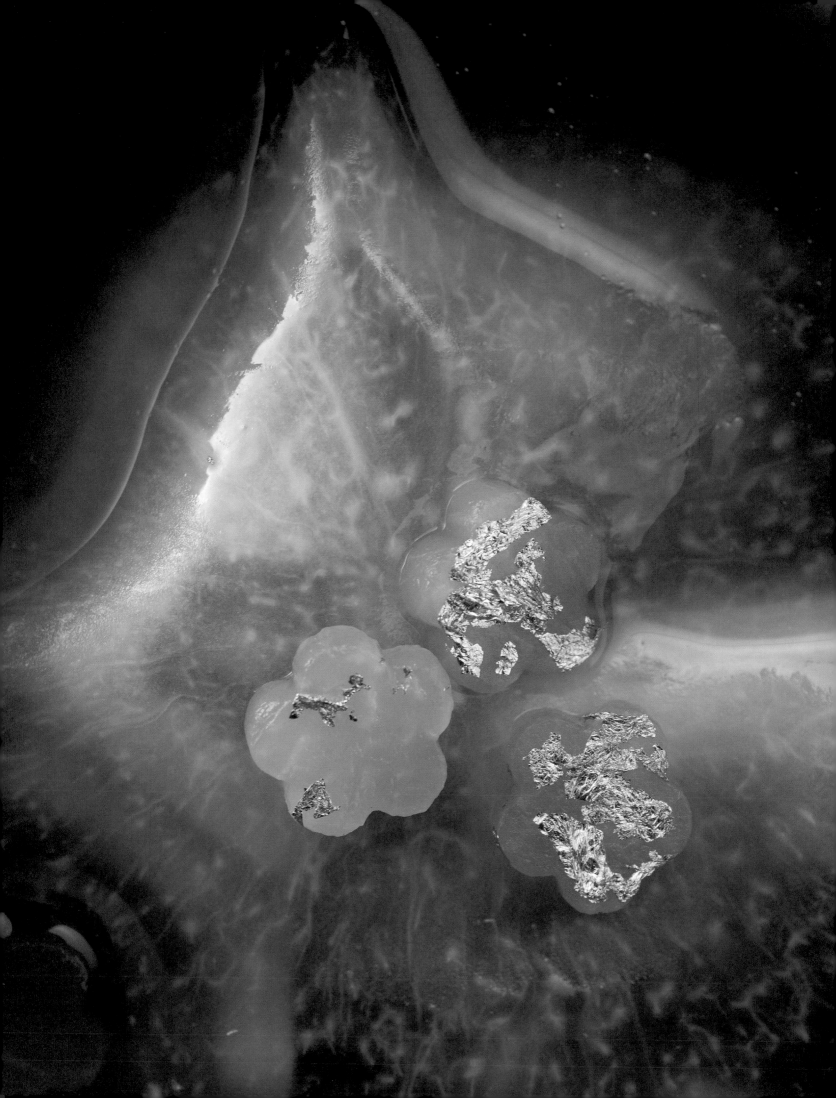

鼈胡麻豆腐薄氷仕立て
Suppon-goma-dofu Usu-gori-jitate

TURTLE SOUP WITH TURNIP "ICE"

The moment of truth for the soup course comes when the customers lift the lid of the bowl. I want that moment to be filled with rising steam and drama. In February when customers lift the lid they are amazed by the sight of what appears to be a thin sheet of ice floating on the hot soup. This *trompe l'oeil* ice is actually a translucent slice of cooked turnip. Waiting under the "ice" is a treasure trove of delicacies in a thickened broth made from snapping turtle. The main point of interest is a dumpling formed of sesame seed tofu and turtle meat. Other garnishes include a votive tablet carved from *kuwai*, a kind of water chestnut, plum-flowers sculpted from root vegetables, seared leeks, and mugwort-scented *kusa mochi*. Every garnish refers to a famous plum blossom festival held at the Kitano Tenmangu Shrine. This soup is a veritable snapshot of February in a bowl, and hints at the coming spring.

煮物椀 February *Nimono-wan*

- *Suppon*/snapping turtle ■ sesame seed tofu ■ Shogoin turnips
- leeks ■ *kuwai*/water chestnut ■ *daikon* ■ carrots
- *kusa mochi*/mugwort rice cake ■ ginger juice ■ gold leaf

recipe p.180

睦月の八寸 *Mutsuki no Hassun*

JANUARY HASSUN

Many customers come to Kikunoi in January expressly to ring in the New Year. So this month's hassun takes its cue from *osechi ryori*, the traditional Japanese New Year's feast. Each item carries a symbolic wish for a happy New Year, and a New Year's meal without them would be as unthinkable for us as a Thanksgiving dinner without a roast turkey and cranberry sauce would be for most Americans.

花弁寿司 *Hanabira-zushi*
FLOWER PETAL SUSHI

This sushi is made of smoked salmon and sushi rice, *gobo* burdock root and carrots wrapped in a thin slice of turnip. It looks like a sweet called *hanabira mochi*, or flower petal rice cakes, which are traditionally served on New Year's Day.

ごまめ結び *Gomame Musubi*
DRIED SARDINES

In this festive dish I toast dried small sardines in a pan and season them with a syrup made from mirin, soy sauce and sugar. Its name is a wish for an abundant rice harvest.

ちしゃとう粕漬け *Chishato Kasu-zuke*
CHISHATO PICKLED IN SAKE LEES

Chishato is a kind of lettuce. Since it is in season and the color is beautiful, I serve it pickled in sake lees.

黒豆松葉刺し *Kuromame Matsuba-zashi*
BLACK SOYBEANS SKEWERED ON PINE NEEDLES

These sweet black soybeans are simmered with sugar. They are a wish for good health so we can work hard in the coming year.

小川からすみ *Ogawa Karasumi*
DRIED MULLET ROE ROLLED WITH SQUID

Dried mullet roe is wrapped in a layer of raw squid then pickled in sake lees.

子持ち昆布 *Komochi Kombu*
KELP WITH HERRING ROE

At New Year's we commonly eat salted herring roe, whose name is a play on words for having many children. Here I've used strips of *kombu* seaweed coated in the roe.

豆慈姑 *Mame Kuwai*
SMALL WATER CHESTNUTS

This dish comprises boiled water chestnuts, or *kuwai*. They are eaten on New Year's in the hope that success will grow like the buds that sprout from their tops. *recipes p.181*

海老芋二種揚げ
Ebi-imo Nishu-age

FRIED EBI-IMO WITH TWO KINDS OF CRUST

Ebi-imo is a traditional Kyoto vegetable. It is a kind of taro whose name means "shrimp potato"—which comes from the shrimp-like striped pattern of the skin. Though I call this dish "fried *ebi-imo*," I consider it to be more of a simmered dish. Usually, aromatic garnishes are not used with fried dishes but in this case I allow myself to sprinkle a little *yuzu* citrus zest on top.

To cook, I simmer the ebi-imo in seasoned *dashi*. The taro is actually ready to eat at this point but to achieve something a little more exciting to serve in my restaurant, I add a contrast in textures. To make the softness of the taro stand out, I coat them in crushed *arare* rice crackers and deep-fry until the outside is crisp. My first attempts at this were a success, but I wanted an even more interesting crust. Then I remembered that my father used to coat foods with poppy seeds and deep-fry them. Arare and poppy seeds have different textures and fragrances, and I find the contrast between them creates a nice rhythm. The crusts are very thin and light and almost greaseless, creating the sensation that this may indeed be a simmered dish.

<hr>

強肴 **December** *Shiizakana*

■ *Ebi-imo*/**shrimp potato** ■ **poppy seeds**
■ *arare* **powder/finely crushed rice crackers** ■ **yuzu zest** *recipe p.181*

鴨鍋
Kamo Nabe

DUCK HOT POT

Many restaurants keep on hand a variety of ceramic vessels to suit different meals, but generally they use the same *shichirin*, or small charcoal brazier, for different meals and different occasions. I can't blame them, because there are few shichirin to choose from in the shops. However, I have my braziers made to order. Presentation is a crucial part of cooking and everything from the choice of plates and utensils, to the appearance of the food and the level of service greatly affect the dining experience. Even if I am serving a simple one-pot meal, commonly cooked on the table at home or in *izakaya* Japanese pubs, I need to give customers something sophisticated. I feel I can only achieve this by coordinating my utensils so that the dish, pot and *shichirin* perfectly complement each other.

Of course, you need to cook something in that beautiful pot on the brazier, and in December it is duck and *Kujo negi*—sweet green winter onions—a favorite Kyoto vegetable. Though this dish is called "duck hot pot," it might be better named "green onion hot pot." These green onions grown in the Takagamine district of Kyoto and are so exquisitely delicious that I created this one-pot dish especially to showcase them.

<hr>

強肴 **December** *Shiizakana*

■ **Duck** ■ *Kujo negi*/**winter green onions**
■ **ground** *sansho* **pepper**
recipe p.182

如月の八寸 *Kisaragi no Hassun*

FEBRUARY HASSUN

February abounds with festivals. As the celebrations follow one after another, almost imperceptibly winter loosens its grip and spring edges closer. The Umehana Matsuri plum blossom festival at Kitano Tenmangu Shrine is a major February event. The shrine is dedicated to Michizane Sugawara, a scholar who, at the age of five, penned this delightful waka poem:

How beautiful the red plum blossom is
I wish to color my cheek with it

In this spirit I've arranged plum-blossom jelly and plum tofu on a votive tablet-shaped plate, which in Japanese is called *ema*, meaning a picture of a horse. There is an equine reference in a piece of rein-shaped sushi, and since we throw beans to ward off demons at another February festival called *Setsubun*, I have scattered a few soybeans around the tray.

手綱寿司　*Tazuna-zushi*
REIN-SHAPED SUSHI
This stick-shaped sushi, decorated to resemble reins,
is composed of slices of marinated sardine, boiled shrimp and
the pungent herb *mitsuba*.

のし梅　*Noshi Ume*
PLUM-FLOWER JELLY
Noshi ume plum jelly is made by a local confectioner and stamped
into the shape of a five-petaled plum flower.

黒豆　*Kuromame*
BLACK SOYBEANS
Black soybeans grown in the Tanba district are simmered
with sugar until tender.

鱈の子落雁　*Tara no Ko Rakugan*
COD ROE CAKES
These steamed cod roe cakes are made from flaked cod roe
mixed with lily bulbs and red Kyoto carrots.

菜の花芥子和え　*Nanohana Karashi-ae*
RAPINI WITH JAPANESE MUSTARD DRESSING
The rapini is quickly blanched and then soaked in dashi seasoned with
soy sauce. Finally I dress it with Japanese mustard.

梅豆腐　*Ume Dofu*
PLUM BLOSSOM TOFU
I season drained tofu in tart plum paste and use a die to
form it into plum-blossom shapes.

ふきのとう味噌漬け　*Fuki no To Miso-zuke*
MISO PICKLED FUKI NO TO
The *fuki no to* are seasoned with miso paste and sprinkled
with cooked egg yolk.

白魚柚香煮　*Shirauo Yuzuka-ni*
COOKED WHITEBAIT WITH YUZU
This dish consists of quickly cooked whitebait in lightly seasoned
dashi, garnished with fragrant yuzu peel.

花山葵　*Hanawasabi*
JAPANESE HORSERADISH BLOSSOMS
Wasabi blossoms mellowed in seasoned dashi　*recipes p.182*

魴鰹南蛮焼き
Managatsuo Nanban-yaki

POMPANO GRILLED NANBAN STYLE

Pompano is caught in the western to southern part of Japan. Although in Japanese its name is derived from *katsuo*—bonito—it is not a kind of bonito at all. In fact, it looks like a giant angel fish. Any fish has an ideal size at which its flavor is at its peak, and in the case of pompano, the bigger it is, the better it tastes. The same goes for Spanish mackerel or halibut. I like to use a pompano that weighs about four and a half pounds (2 kilos). The meat is full flavored and stands up well to *nanban*-style grilling. I marinate it in sake, mirin, light soy sauce and salt, and add some chopped onions, ginger, and *yuzu* peel. After the fish comes out of the marinade I sprinkle on more onions, ginger and yuzu. I'm aiming for an aroma that is robust and vivid, so that when you bite into the grilled pompano and crush the bits of ginger and yuzu with your teeth, the zesty fragrance grows. This yakimono also includes scallops that are lightly grilled then dusted with just-toasted *karasumi* dry-cured mullet roe. The salty roe enhances the flavor of the rare-cooked scallops.

As for the serving vessel, I actually made it myself during a visit to a ceramic artist in Bizen, Okayama Prefecture. I wasn't looking to create a masterpiece, I was just enjoying myself, playing with the clay and this is what emerged.

焼物 February *Yakimono*

■ *Managatsuo/Pompano* ■ onions ■ ginger ■ yuzu ■ scallops
■ *karasumi/dried mullet roe* ■ *amigasa yuzu*
recipe p.183

穴子飯蒸し
Anago Ii-mushi

SEA EEL WITH RICE

I have to admit I adore *anago* sea eel. Most people believe it has a very light and delicate taste, and while it is true that it could be classed as delicate, I contend it is actually quite richly flavored. What I mean is it has a great depth of *umami*—the "fifth taste" after sweet, sour, salty and bitter. Umami is hard to translate but might be characterized as "meaty," "savory," or even having qualities of natural deliciousness. Foods like anchovies, cheese, soy sauce and tomatoes are said to strongly exhibit umami. It is very important in Japanese cuisine, because it allows us to create depth of flavor without using heavy oils or cream. Anago is useful in this respect, and I put it in the *hirosu* and *Toji-maki* recipes to boost those dishes.

To make sea eel with rice, I simmer anago fillets in a sweet and salty sauce until they are tender. I cook the glutinous rice in similar seasonings, then steam it again folded in eel fillets. The tender sea eel is almost bursting with umami as it disintegrates in your mouth and the rice is sticky and warm. Eating doesn't get much better than this.

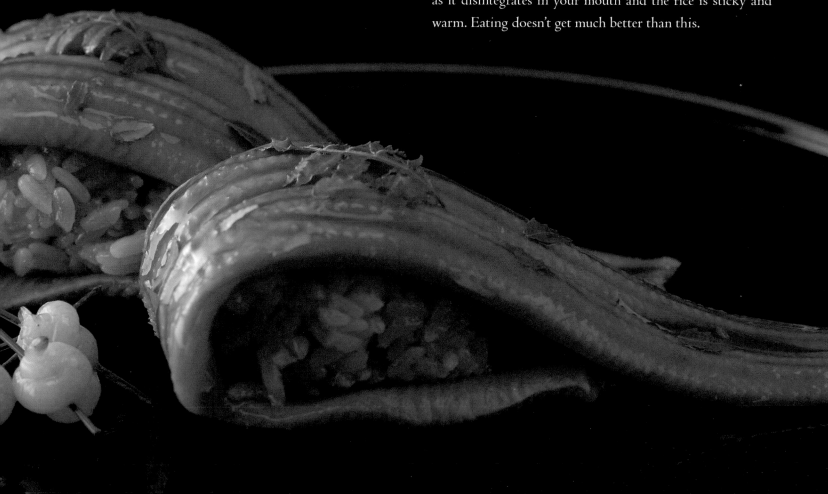

御飯 February *Gohan*

■ Sea eels ■ glutinous rice ■ chopped *kinome* leaf buds
■ *chorogi*   recipe p.183

汲み上げ湯葉このわた蒸し
Kumiage Yuba Konowata-mushi

KUMIAGE YUBA AND SEA CUCUMBER ROE

BOTTOM: December

きんこ蒸し　*Kinko-mushi*

STEAMED SEA CUCUMBER

CENTER: February

赤飯蒸し　*Sekihan-mushi*

RED RICE

TOP: January

In colder months, four hot sakizuke are served to help ward off the chill. Beginning with *kumoko-mushi* in November and continuing to these three dishes in December, January and February, I take great pains to create a warm welcome. The small striped dish in the photo contains steamed *kumiage yuba* and sea cucumber roe. Kumiage yuba is like a thickened cream of soy milk; on top of that rests dried *konoko*, sea cucumber ovaries, and at the bottom there is *konowata*, salted sea cucumber entrails. Its flavor is deeply redolent of the ocean, and I've used it here in the same way the Italians use anchovies as a seasoning. The yuba and konowata share a creamy texture that is out of this world.

The resulting combination is dense and powerfully flavored—a little goes a long way. *Kinko-mushi* (center) is very rich as well. Kinko is dried sea cucumber, and in the olden days it was literally worth its weight in gold. (In fact the "kin" in its name comes from the Japanese word for gold.) Its taste is austere, but it is sought after for its gelatinous texture and purported medicinal qualities. I perk it up a bit by steaming it together with *konowata* and bathe it in *gin-an* sauce. Its elegant aroma reminds me of the winter ocean. The top dish, *sekihan-mushi*, is not as rich as the others. Sekihan, steamed glutinous rice with red beans, is a favorite dish at celebrations because red and white are considered to be auspicious colors. I need a more elaborate version for my restaurant so I cook the steamed rice with sake and salt, then I decorate it with kumiage yuba, *bekko-an*, a soy-based sauce, fresh sea urchin roe and *wasabi*.

先付　**Winter *Sakizuke***

BOTTOM
- *Kumiage yuba* ▪ *konowata*
- *arare konoko*/dried konoko

CENTER
- *Kinko* ▪ *konowata* ▪ *gin-an*/silver sauce
- ginger juice ▪ chives

TOP
- *Sekihan* (steamed glutinous rice with red beans)
- *kumiage yuba* ▪ fresh sea urchin roe
- *uguisuna*/greens ▪ grated *wasabi*
- *bekko-an*/amber sauce　*recipes p.183*

御造り *Otsukuri*

Sashimi

鰧 *Okoze*

SCORPION FISH

We have a saying: "poisonous fish are delicious." Our fatal attraction to *fugu* blowfish is well known, but we also enjoy *okoze*, scorpion fish, the poisonous dorsal spines of which can cause a careless cook's hands to swell to twice their normal size. The okoze looks ferocious, but makes very good eating; in fact, I prefer it to blowfish. *Okoze* is in season during summer, but tastes better in winter, when it is found in the cold ocean depths.

Like fugu, okoze sashimi is usually thinly sliced, using a technique called *usu-zukuri*. I don't like it too thin, so I slice a little thicker for more substantial texture. I also want my customers to enjoy the skin and stomach, which I boil and cut into strips. The smooth, slightly buttery flavor of the entrails and the refined taste of the sliced meat is a fabulous combination. As I have said before, good otsukuri is dependent on the skillful use of knives. High-quality blades must be well honed and maintained, and the same goes for the skills of the chef handling them. However, while the tools and skills are important, the mental component is paramount. You need to use your imagination and consider what you would like to express through your culinary handiwork.

向付 **Winter *Mukozuke***

■ *Okoze*/scorpion fish ■ *pon-zu*/vinegar with citrus ■ chives
recipe p.184

伊勢海老 *Ise Ebi*

SPINY LOBSTER

Whereas for the summer otsukuri course I prepare shrimp by boiling them for two seconds, here I cut the spiny lobster into pieces and swirl them vigorously in ice water. This cleans and firms the meat. The fresher the lobster, the more the muscle fibers contract, and the sweet, juicy flavors naturally burst forth.

向付 Winter *Mukozuke*

■ **Spiny lobster** ■ grated *wasabi* ■ **Tosa soy sauce**
recipe p.184

鮪 *Maguro Toro*

FATTY TUNA

I use locally caught *maguro* for this sashimi. The balance of fat to red meat in the *toro*—the fatty meat—is the best. By using a variety of different cuts, I can emphasize different aspects of the tuna. When a customer takes a piece of toro, I want it almost to melt in the mouth. To emphasize this soft, buttery texture, I cut it into long, thin pieces. As for the *akami*, the red meat of the same tuna, I make the cuts a little shorter and thicker to let customers enjoy the chewy texture. I hope you will try this sashimi with Japanese mustard and *kimi-joyu* soy sauce mixed with egg yolks. I soak the egg yolks in soy sauce for about two days, then whisk. Though it might sound a little unusual, the richness of the tuna is complemented by the thickly unctuous yolks.

向付 Winter *Mukozuke*

■ **Tuna** ■ **egg yolk soy sauce** ■ **dissolved Japanese mustard** *recipe p.184*

鮒鰹奉書焼き
Managatsuo Hosho-yaki

PAPILLOTE OF POMPANO

Wrapping food before cooking is an effective way to seal in flavor and moisture. In Kyoto we often marinate fish in miso paste before broiling it. Pompano prepared this way is delicious, but it tends to dry out on the grill. To get around this problem, I came up with the idea to wrap it in wet *hosho* paper and bake it in an oven. The fish looks better with a little color so I brown it before wrapping. I've fleshed out the dish with some symbolic garnishes: clams represent happiness and the golden color of cooked kumquats symbolizes prosperity. Also, the kumquat's sweet and sour taste is an excellent palate refresher.

焼物 **January** *Yakimono*

- **■ *Managatsuo*/pompano ■ *miso yuanji*/marinade**
- **■ clams ■ kumquats** *recipe p.184*

蕪蒸し　*Kabura-mushi*

STEAMED TURNIPS

Kabura mushi is one of the most typical Kyoto winter dishes. There are as many versions of these steamed turnips as there are restaurants, and each chef tries to put their own stamp on it.

At Kikunoi, each generation has served its own unique version. My dish is totally different from my grandfather's and my father's. The dining room was much colder in the old days and customers needed a heavy, stick-to-the-ribs dish to warm them up. We have central heating now so I'm able to use a lighter touch. I whisk egg whites to make a soufflé of turnips that's soft and light as powdered snow. Tilefish contributes flavor and *kikurage* cloud ear mushrooms, ginkgo nuts and lily bulbs provide textural interest. This delicate assemblage is topped off with a dollop of fresh sea urchin roe, slightly thickened silver sauce and a pungent dab of *wasabi*. I wonder what the customers of old would think of this lighter, twenty-first-century version of steamed turnips.

蓋物　December *Futamono*

■ **Turnips** ■ **Wakasa tilefish** ■ **ginkgo nuts**
■ *kikurage*/**cloud ear mushrooms** ■ **lily bulbs** ■ **egg whites**
■ **fresh sea urchin roe** ■ *gin-an*/**silver sauce** ■ **grated** *wasabi*
recipe p.184

ふかひれ鍋　*Fukahire Nabe*

SHARK FIN HOT POT

Chinese shark fin dishes are often swimming in a thickened sauce. I've usually found the sauce to be good, but the actual shark fin is a little bland. By itself, shark fin has a lot more texture than taste, not unlike Japan's *konnyaku*—a tasteless, firm, vegetable jelly—which, when simmered, easily absorbs other flavors. I thought that if I simmered the shark fin in a strong *suppon* snapping turtle soup, it would infuse the fins with flavor. After a successful test, I put together a robustly flavored shark fin hot pot using snapping turtle soup, turtle meat, sesame seed tofu, grilled green onion, and finally shark fin that had been simmered and steeped in turtle soup. Since I use a fair amount of sake in the soup, I chose a *junmai godanjikomi* type which is brewed from pure rice in five steps, instead of the normal three. It has about twice the amount of amino acids as regular sake, which gives the soup a deep, meaty flavor.

強肴　January *Shiizakana*

■ **Shark fin** ■ *suppon*/**snapping turtle** ■ **sesame seed tofu**
■ **grilled onions** ■ **ginger** ■ **sake**　*recipe p.184*

焼き松葉蟹
Yaki Matsuba-gani

GRILLED SNOW CRABS

Matsuba-gani, snow crab, is truly the king of crabs. The best way to cook one is to grill it over charcoal. Before your eyes, the translucent meat swells and lifts away from the shell. The first bite, unsalted and unadorned, will give you the real taste of crab. Of course boiled crabs are mighty good too, but the grilled ones taste sweeter and have more essential crab flavor.

Many ingredients from nature possess great beauty, including snow crabs. We pursue them to the very depths of the ocean in order to eat them. Since we take their lives, we owe it to them to prepare them properly and with respect. I am often touched by the sublime beauty of freshly picked vegetables or live seafood. I owe them nothing less than my best efforts.

焼物　December *Yakimono*

■ *Matsuba-gani*/snow crab
recipe p.185

てっぱい *Teppai*

SQUID AND SCALLIONS WITH MISO DRESSING

One of the most popular spring dishes is *nuta*, a traditional food usually made from scallions and seasonal shellfish tossed in a miso and rice-vinegar dressing that often contains hot Japanese mustard. We call it *teppai* in Kyoto, because long ago, a chef observed that the central flowering stalk of the *wakegi* scallion looked like a bullet emerging from the barrel of a *teppo*, or pistol. Dishes using scallions and mixed dressings were called *teppo-ae*, which came to be pronounced *teppai*. Indeed, so involved is the etymology of this dish that even Japanese from other regions would be clueless as to what teppai might be if they saw the word on a menu.

Kikunoi's teppai combines blanched scallions and grilled squid with sake and *Omi konnyaku*. I chose squid instead of the usual shellfish because I wanted a more subtle taste. Omi konnyaku is a bright red vegetable gelatin that adds an interesting note of color and texture. I also add *daidai*—bitter orange—juice to the white miso dressing for a refreshing, light citrus taste. A garnish of julienned, dried daidai peel, known as *chinpi*, provides a seasonal touch.

酢肴 **February** *Su-zakana*

■ *Wakegi*/scallions ■ squid ■ *Omi konnyaku* ■ *Saikyo miso*
■ Japanese mustard ■ *rice vinegar* ■ *daidai* juice ■ *chinpi* of
daidai/julienne of daidai peel

recipe p.185

百合根饅頭
Yurine Manju

LILY BULB DUMPLINGS

Kyoto cooking is tradition-bound; sometimes this is a good thing and other times it is better to move ahead. For instance, this simple dish of ground meat wrapped in a paste of steamed lily bulbs takes an inordinate amount of time to make by hand. To prepare a sufficient quantity for a restaurant requires two strong cooks to spend a long time laboring over a huge mortar and pestle, to mash the ingredients to a smooth consistency. I found that a food processor makes the job much easier. It was over twenty years ago, and people were shocked that I was using a food processor for Japanese cuisine. But I think cooking should follow the dictates of reason, and if I can achieve the same results using a food processor instead of a mortar, I will use the machine without hesitation. If I can avoid unnecessary work, I can concentrate on more important aspects of cooking.

I often serve these lily dumplings at international food events and they are delicious with an elegant truffle sauce in place of the usual *kinome* sauce. Even dressed up in truffle sauce I still think they can be called *washoku*, Japanese cooking.

蓋物 January *Futamono*

■ **Lily bulbs** ■ *jinenjo*/**Japanese yams** ■ *joshinko*/**rice flour**
■ **quails** ■ **foie gras** ■ *aomi daikon*/**green radish** ■ **red carrots**
■ *kinome* **leaf bud sauce**
recipe p.185

雪鍋　*Yuki Nabe*

SNOWY HOT POT

In my early thirties I sat in Zen meditation with Seiko Hirata Roshi, now the chief abbot at Tenryuji Temple. I wasn't really looking for enlightenment; I just enjoyed spending time with him and listening to his stories. One day he offered to cook, saying, "You always treat me to nice food, so it's my treat this time." It was a freezing day at the beginning of spring, and the meal appeared to be a block of tofu in a huge, rugged earthenware pot. He said, "Just a second," then opened the door and went to the garden to pick some *fuki no to* coltsfoot buds, which he threw into the tofu pot.

There were other dishes: tender-boiled *daikon* radish, and *nanohana* rapini dressed with Japanese mustard. The master pointed outside and said, "The daikon was grown in that field, and the rapini was brought by a novice monk from over there." When we had finished eating, I asked, "What was today's teaching?" He replied, "I just wanted to cook you a good meal. Temple food is not bad, is it?" I couldn't figure out why this august personage would just casually prepare a meal for someone like me, and I chased this thought through my mind until it dawned on me that he may have been telling me to think about cooking in a more simple and fundamental way.

About ten years later, when I found the opportunity to thank the Roshi for his guidance, he just looked at me and said: "Hmm. I don't remember that at all."

That's the way Zen masters are, I guess. I still keep his lesson in mind.

February's simple snow pot reflects Hirata Roshi's teaching. I got the idea from a scene of falling sleet in the early spring. What looks like sleet in this pot is grated daikon. I cook tilefish and tofu in *dashi* and add the daikon at the last moment before serving. It's a good way to enjoy daikon that has been sweetened by winter frosts.

強肴　**February Shiizakana**

■ **Grated radish** ■ **tilefish** ■ **tofu** ■ *kikuna*/**chrysanthemum leaves**
■ *arare yuzu*/**diced yuzu** ■ *fuki no to*/**coltsfoot buds**
recipe p.185

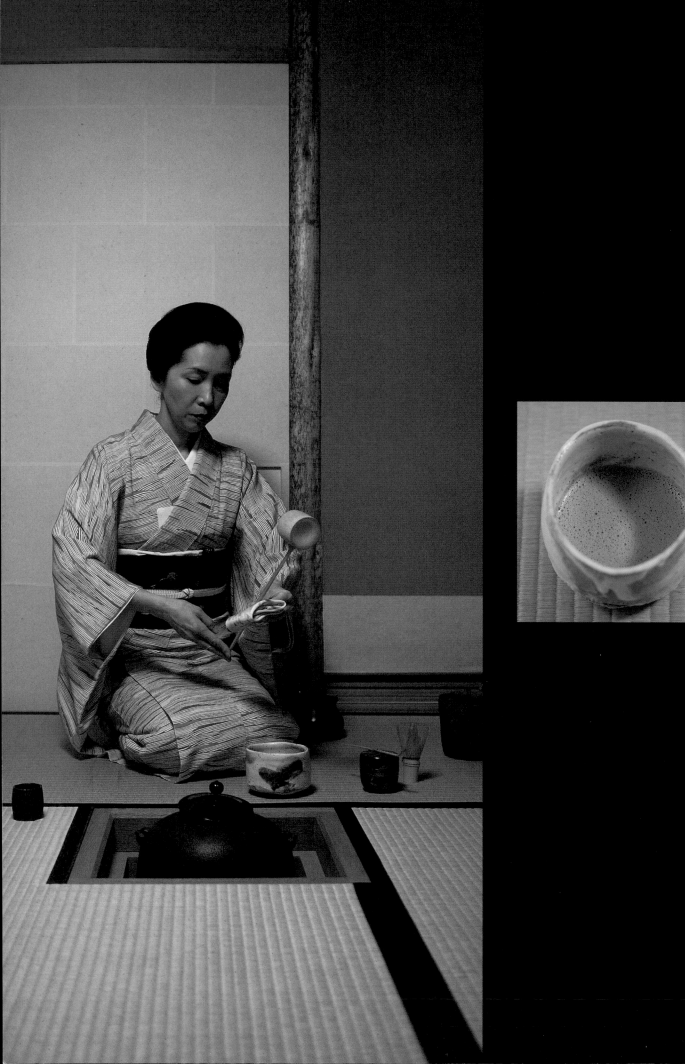

冬の水物　*Fuyu no Mizumono*

WINTER MIZUMONO

We Japanese cooks often fret about the borderline between Japanese and other cuisines. For example, we endlessly question whether a certain amount of butter will make a dish "Western," or if it is only a small amount, will the dish still be "Japanese?" The irony, I am sure, is that customers couldn't care less. If a piece of cake is good, they will eat it with relish and lick the fork when they are done. I am not saying, "anything goes." What I mean is that a cook must always bear in mind the essence of deliciousness. This is the real nature of Japanese cuisine, and innovation won't work without the conscious pursuit of this essence.

The winter desserts I would like to introduce are *kinkan* kumquat sorbet, fruit jelly, and a special Japanese-style sweet. Since kumquats have a tangy aroma and their skin is soft and not too bitter, I often simmer them whole with sugar. But the flavor of kumquat is too strong in a normal sorbet, so I add some yogurt to make it smoother. As for the fruit jelly, I add only a touch of gelatin so as to barely harden it, which is the style I like. Finally I serve a sweet to accompany *matcha* green tea. These cakes go by the poetic name *yuki-mochi matsu*, meaning "pine trees covered in snow." They are made from a green, sweet-bean paste wrapped in a skin of grated yams and rice flour, then steamed. The green filling represents pine trees and the white outside layer represents snow.

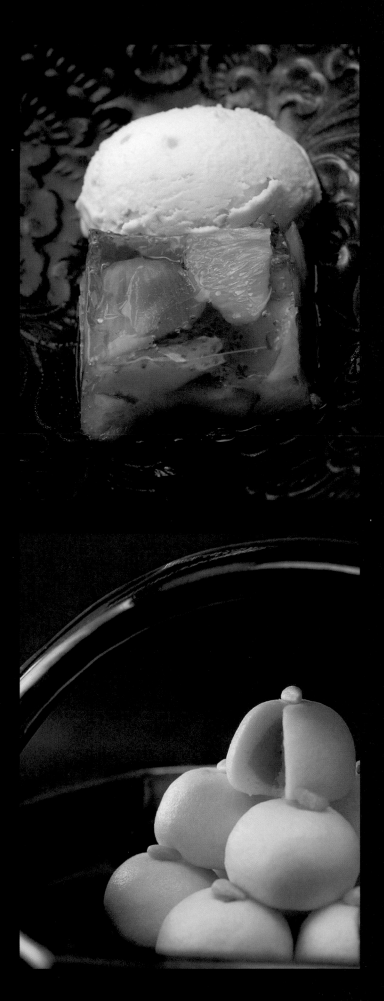

金柑ソルベ　*Kinkan Sorbet*
KUMQUAT SORBET
■ **Kumquats** ■ **granulated sugar** ■ **plain yogurt**
recipe p.186

フルーツゼリー　*Fruit Jelly*
FRUIT JELLY
■ **Strawberries** ■ **Kiwi fruit** ■ **oranges** ■ **granulated sugar**
■ **pearl agar** ■ **Chinese osmanthus flower liqueur**
recipe p.186

雪持ち松　*Yuki-mochi Matsu*
SNOWY DUMPLINGS
■ *yamaimo*/**mountain yams** ■ **rice flour**
■ **sweet bean paste** ■ **pine nuts**
recipes p.186

ABOUT *DASHI*

When it comes to kaiseki, there can be no avoiding a discussion on the subject of *dashi*, the simple stock based on dried bonito flakes. Almost every dish is built on a foundation of dashi. Although there are many variations, its fundamental ingredients are *kombu* kelp, dried bonito flakes and water. Kombu contains amino acids such as glutamic acid and aspartic acid and dried bonito flakes contain inosinic acid. In combination these flavor-enhacing acids act to amplify the *umami* flavor in any dish. This stock is so essential that I cannot imagine kaiseki without it.

I would like to outline the important elements and share my stock making techniques with any would-be kaiseki chefs.

METHOD

A new method has dramatically changed the way dashi has been made for centuries. Traditionally we put the kombu in water and take 30 minutes to bring it to a boil. But scientific observation has shown that the glutamic acid in kombu cannot be extracted over 176°F (80°C). So it is meaningless to raise the temperature any higher. And it has been proven that the optimum temperature for extraction is 140°F (60°C). I have conducted many experiments to discover the best way to extract only a clear umami taste without any trace of fishy smell or bitterness. Although my way of making dashi differs from previous methods, I believe it is the best way.

Making Dashi

1. Wipe the surface of a 1oz (30g) piece of kombu with a moist towel.
2. Combine 1.8 liters soft water and the kombu from step 1 in a pan on very low heat. Slowly raise the temperature to 140°F (60°C) and extract the umami of the kombu by holding that temperature for one hour.
3. Remove the kombu and, taking care not to boil, raise the temperature to 176°F (80°C). Turn off the heat and immediately add 1²/₃oz (50g) of shaved dried bonito flakes.
4. When the dried bonito flakes are soaked, leave them for about 10 seconds and strain through a fine sieve covered with cheese cloth. Never squeeze the bonito flakes; just let the liquid drain naturally.

Water

Soft water is essential to making *dashi*. It is impossible to extract the glutamic acid from kombu with water that has a hardness of more than 60 parts-per-million of calcium carbonate. If your water is harder than this, the only option is to use softened water or soft bottled water. The taste of the water is also important. The name Kikunoi means Chrysanthemum Well, and our family crest features a chrysanthemum surrounded by a well. We don't use the original well, but ever since we opened our first restaurant, we have always used similar water, pumped from 453 feet (138m) underground. The taste of the water is so impor-

tant that I even send it from Kyoto to my restaurant in Akasaka, Tokyo. The water is one ingredient that you just can't compromise on.

Kombu

I use first-grade Rishiri kombu that has been cultivated in Kabuka Bay at Rebun Island, Hokkaido, in northern Japan. It is dried naturally and stored in a humidity- and temperature-controlled warehouse for more than one year. The top grade of Rishiri kombu is a rare treasure. My supplier obtains this precious kombu from fishermen and ages it to make it the best quality kombu available. Because of our longstanding relationship, whenever I give them a call, they send only the amount I need right then, so I always have access to the best kombu in its top condition.

Dried bonito flakes

The dried bonito flakes that I use come from blocks of dried bonito called *honbushi* made in Makurazaki, Kagoshima in southern Japan. It is *obushi*, made from the dorsal fillets and aged for about one year. No matter how good the dried bonito is, if you don't use it immediately after it has been shaved, its aroma and flavor will be ruined.

BASIC RECIPES

Ground Walnuts

Bake walnuts in a 300°F (150°C) oven until well browned and put them through a meat grinder, or grind them with a Japanese mortar and pestle until the oil oozes out. Unsweetened walnut paste can be substituted for this recipe.

Ground Sesame Seeds

Put toasted sesame seeds through a meat grinder or, grind them with a Japanese mortar and pestle until the oil oozes out to make a paste. Prepared sesame seed paste can be substituted for this recipe.

Tosa-zu   YIELDS ABOUT 1 1/4 cups (300ml)

1 cup (225ml) *dashi*
5 Tablespoons (75ml) vinegar
1 Tablespoon light soy sauce
1/2 teaspoon sugar
1/3oz (10g) dried bonito flakes

Heat dashi, vinegar, light soy sauce and sugar in a pan. Just before it boils, add dried bonito flakes and turn off heat. Let cool, strain.

Tosa-zu Jelly   YIELDS ABOUT 4/5 cup (200ml)

4/5 cup (200ml) *Tosa-zu*
1/2 teaspoon (2.5g) gelatin powder

Gently heat tosa-zu and gelatin powder in a pan. When the gelatin dissolves, take off the stove, and pour into a 8.5"/21cm square pan, refrigerate overnight and strain through a sieve.

Miso Yuanji   YIELDS ABOUT 2.9lbs (1.3k)

2.2lbs (1k) *Saikyo miso* sweet white miso paste
Miso stock
(3/4 cup (175ml) sake, 3/4 cup (175ml) water, 3 Tablespoons *mirin*, 2 teaspoons light soy sauce, 4 teaspoons regular soy sauce)
1/2 *yuzu* peel without pith

1. Bring a stock in a pan to boil and vaporize the alcohol. Let cool.
2. Chop yuzu skin.
3. Combine 1 1/2 cups (350ml) of stock with sweet white miso paste, add yuzu skin and mix well.

Pon-zu   YIELDS ABOUT 16oz (450ml)

Vinegar with Citrus   FOR RAW SEAFOOD

3/4 cup (180ml) lemon juice
1/5 cup (50ml) sake
1/5 cup (50ml) *mirin*
1 Tablespoon water
1/3 cup (80ml) regular soy sauce
1 Tablespoon light soy sauce
2/3oz (20g) *kombu*
1/3 (10g) dried bonito flakes

1. Soak kombu in lemon juice for about a half day.
2. Combine sake, mirin, light soy sauce, regular soy sauce and water and boil until alcohol in sake and mirin evaporates. Add dried bonito flakes and let cool. Stain.
3. Remove the kombu from the lemon juice from step 1 and combine with the stock from step 2.

Shime-zu   YIELDS ABOUT 2 1/2 cups (570ml)

Pickling Vinegar   FOR FISH

1.9 cups (450ml) rice vinegar
5 Tablespoons sugar
5 Tablespoons light soy sauce

Bring vinegar, sugar and light soy sauce to a boil. When sugar dissolves, turn off the heat and let cool.

Ama-zu   YIELDS ABOUT 1qt (1l)

Sweetened Vinegar

4/5 cup (200ml) rice vinegar
2 1/2 cups (600ml) water
9 Tablespoons sugar
1/3oz (7g) *kombu*

1. Combine vinegar, water and sugar, add kombu and let sit for a day.
2. Heat the mixture from step 1 in a pan and when it starts to boil, turn off the heat. Let cool, then remove kombu.

Kikka no Tosa-zu-zuke

Chrysanthemum Blossoms Pickled in Tosa-zu

Separate the petals from chrysanthemum flowers and blanch them in boiling water with vinegar. Plunge into ice water, then soak in *Tosa-zu*.

Sushi Rice   YIELDS ABOUT 3 3/4 cups (900ml)

1 1/2 cup (360ml) rice
1 1/2 cup (360ml) water
1 sheet 1 3/4" (4cm) kombu
4 Tablespoons *sushi-zu* sushi vinegar (see recipe below)

1. Wash rice in 2 or three changes of cold water and let drain in a sieve 30 minutes before cooking. Combine kombu, water and rice in a rice cooker and steam.
2. Let the just-cooked rice rest for 10 minutes and transfer to a tub. Pour the sushi vinegar over the rice and mix with a rice paddle using a gentle slicing and tossing motion.

Sushi-zu   YIELDS ABOUT 1/2 cup (120ml)

Sushi Vinegar for Non-raw-fish Sushi

Taste may vary depending on the quality of seasonings.
1/2 cup (120ml) rice vinegar (*Chidori-su*, a brand of mild rice vinegar from Kyoto)

2/3oz (20g) sea salt (*Umi no sei*)
6 1/4 Tablespoons (75g) sugar

Combine all of the ingredients in a pan and bring to a boil. Mix well and when salt and sugar dissolve, remove from the heat.
The proper amount of this sushi vinegar for 3/4 cup (180ml) of uncooked rice is about 2 Tablespoons.

Sushi-zu   YIELDS ABOUT 2 1/2 cups (600ml)

Sushi Vinegar for Raw-fish Sushi

This sushi vinegar is used for sushi with raw fish ingredients such as the *hassun* course.
1 1/2 cups (360ml) rice vinegar (*Chidori-su*)
1 1/4 cups (240g) sugar
6 Tablespoons (90g) sea salt (*Umi no sei*)

Combine all of the ingredients in a pan and bring to a boil until salt and sugar dissolve.
The proper amount of this sushi vinegar for 3/4 cup (180ml) of uncooked rice is 2 Tablespoons.

Kuzu

At Kikunoi, Yoshino's hon-kuzu (high-quality, pure *kuzu* powder) is usually indicated for "dissolved *kuzu*." However for thicker sauces or items like "sesame seed tofu", Kumagawa's hon-kuzu is used.

Tosa-joyu   YIELDS ABOUT 1 cup (225ml)

Tosa Soy Sauce

5 Tablespoons (75ml) regular soy sauce
1/5 cup (150ml) sake
1/6oz (5g) dried bonito flakes
1 2"/5cm square oiece of Kombu

1. Combine sake, regular soy sauce and kombu in a pan and bring to a boil to let the alcohol evaporate.
2. Put dried bonito flakes and turn off the heat. Let cool, strain.

Taki-miso   YIELDS ABOUT 1lb (500g)

Cooked *miso* paste

1lb (500g) white miso paste
2 1/4 cups (540ml) sake

Add sake to white miso paste and mix well to dissolve miso. Put in a pan over heat and stir with a wooden spoon, taking care not to burn, simmer until the mixture returns to the original thickness of the white miso paste.

RECITES

SPRING

March *Sakizuke* ***Kakure Ume***   P. 16

Hidden Ume   SERVES 10

10 *umeboshi* pickled Japanese plums (large and top quality ones)
3 1/3 cups (800ml) *dashi*
"A" Stock (4 teaspoons light soy sauce and 3/4 teaspoon (4g) salt)
Dried bonito flakes; as needed

Shirako cream

1lb (500g) *Tai no shirako* sea bream milt (very fresh ones)
A pinch of salt
A little sake
A little *atari goma* toasted and ground sesame seeds
"B" stock (4/5 cups (200ml) *dashi*, 1 teaspoon light soy sauce, 1/2 teaspoon *mirin*, and a pinch of salt)

10 *tsukushi* horsetail shoots
Vegetable oil for frying
A dash of salt

1. After pricking the whole surface of the umeboshi with a toothpick or pin, simmer them gently in fresh water on very low heat to remove the salt.

2. Add "A" stock ingredients to dashi and adjust the taste (depending on the saltiness of the umeboshi), and add the umeboshi from step 1. Next, add the dried bonito flakes (*oi-gatsuo*) and simmer on low heat until the plums absorb some of its flavor. Remove from the heat and chill the plums in the stock.

3. Sprinkle the milt with a pinch of salt and let it rest for 1 hour. Sprinkle with a little sake, put it in a bowl and cook in a steamer for 10–15 minutes. Let cool, strain the milt through a fine sieve and add toasted and ground sesame seeds. Grind with a Japanese mortar and pestle until smooth. Adjust the thickness with a little "B" stock and cook in a non-reactive sauce pan over low heat until the milt cream thickens

4. Deep-fry the tips of horsetails and lightly sprinkle with salt.

5. Pour the soft milt cream over the umeboshi and top with horsetail tips for garnish.

■ April *Hassun*

Tai Kinome-zushi   P. 18

Sea Bream and Kinome Sushi   SERVES 8

2.8oz (80g) piece of sea bream fillet
7oz (200g) sushi rice (see basic recipes)
8 *kinome* leaf buds
1 6" (15cm) long piece of *shiroita kombu*, a thin sheet of kelp
Sweetened vinegar (see basic recipes)
Pickling vinegar (see basic recipes)

1. Soak shiroita kombu in sweetened vinegar.

2. Soak the sea bream fillet in vinegar for about 30 minutes. Remove the skin and cut it into 0.28oz to 0.35oz (8 to 10g) slices.

3. When the sushi rice is cooled, combine some chopped kinome leaf buds and shape into a stick.

4. Place the fish slices from step 2 on a wet tea towel and place the rice from step 3 on top. Wrap them in the towel and roll and lightly compress it into a stick-shaped piece of sushi.

5. Sprinkle with the kinome leaf buds on the sushi from step 4 and top with the drained shiroita kombu from step 1.

6. Cut the sushi from step 5 into 8 pieces.

Hanabira Udo

Petal-Shaped Udo

1 3" (7.5cm) piece of *udo* stalk

Cut the udo into a petal shape, thinly slice and soak in water to clean. Drain and put into fresh water with a few drops of red food coloring to dye pink.

Hanami Dango

Dumplings for Cherry-blossom Viewing

Prepare medium shrimp, abalone and avocado according to the following recipe and skewer them to resemble *hanami dango* on about 12cm-length sticks.

Shrimps

2 *kuruma ebi* medium shrimp
Mixed stock (3/4 cup (180ml) sake, 4 teaspoons light soy sauce and 4 teaspoons *mirin*)

1. Remove the heads and devein shrimp. Run a skewer along their length to keep them straight during cooking.

2. Put the mixed stock items into a pan, bring to a boil and when it boils, add the shrimp from step 1. When the color changes, quickly remove and cool on a rack. Cool the stock, soak the shrimps in the cooled stock.

3. After the shrimps have absorbed the stock's flavor, peel them and cut into 1/2" (1.5cm) lengths.

Abalone

1 abalone
3.5oz (100g) *daikon* chunks
1 qt (1l) sake
1 qt (1l) water
4 teaspoons light soy sauce
2 teaspoons *mirin*

1. Scrub abalone with salt and take out from the shell. Rinse and remove the frilly portion.

2. Combine the big chunks of daikon, abalone, sake and water in a pot and cover with a drop lid. When it boils, skim any foam and slowly simmer on medium heat for about 2 hours. Just before it is done, add light soy sauce and mirin and simmer for ten more minutes or until the liquid is completely reduced.

3. Let the Abalone cool, cut into 1/2" (1.5 cm) cubes.

Avocado

1 avocado
A little rice vinegar
7oz (200g) Saikyo *miso* coarse white miso paste

1. Cut an avocado in half lengthwise and remove the seed, and use a melon baller to scoop out balls.

2. Add some vinegar to boiling water, blanch the avocado balls and and plunge them into ice water. Drain on a towel.

3. Spread the white miso paste on a piece of cheese cloth and put avocado balls on top, wrap the balls in the cheese cloth and coat with more miso. Let cure for about 12 hours.

Hanabira Yurine

Lily Bulb Petals

1/2 *yurine* lily bulb
2/3oz (20g) *nama ikura* fresh salmon roe
Stock for salmon roe (3 Tablespoons *nikiri zake*, 3 tablespoons water, 1/2 teaspoon light soy sauce, 1 teaspoon regular soy sauce and 1 teaspoon *mirin*)
Some dried bonito flakes

1. Combine the stock ingredients in a pan, bring to a boil and add dried bonito flakes, turn off the heat, let cool and strain.

2. Soak the salmon roe in the stock from step 1.

3. Steam the lily bulb until done. Sprinkle with a little salt and let cool.

4. Drain the salmon roe and spoon onto a lily bulb "petal."

Iidako

Small Octopus

3 *iidako* small octopus
Stock (1 1/2 cups (360ml) water, 2 Tablespoons light soy sauce, 2 Tablespoons regular soy sauce, 3 Tablespoons *mirin* and 4 teaspoons (15g) sugar)

1. Rinse small octopus and cut off the head and tentacles. Blanch them quickly in boiling water, remove and remove ink sac.

2. Bring stock to a boil. Lower heat and add only the heads, cook for 30 minutes. Cook tentacles the same way for 5 minutes, then let the cooked octopus cool.

3. Let the stock cool. When cooled, steep the heads and tentacles in the stock.

4. When they have absorbed the flavor of the stock, cut into bite-size pieces.

Issun Mame

Broad Beans   SERVES 4

8 *soramame* broad beans (fava beans)
Mixed stock (3/4 cup (180ml) *dashi*, 1 teaspoon light soy sauce, 1 teaspoon *mirin* and 1/5 teaspoon (1g) salt)

1. Remove the beans from the pod and peel.

2. Bring stock to a boil in a small pan. When it boils, quickly cook the peeled beans and remove. Let them cool on a rack. Let the stock cool and steep the beans in the cooled stock.

Warabi Ika
Broiled Squid   SERVES 4

1 6"×2" (15cm×5cm) *mongo ika* cuttlefish tube
1 egg yolk
Aonori dried green *nori* seaweed powder; as needed

1. Rinse squid and slice into ¼" (5mm) thick fillets.

2. To imitate *warabi* bracken fern shoots, roll one side and skewer and broil.

3. Brush with egg yolk and broil again, taking care not to burn the surface. Dust the surface with dried seaweed powder and cut into bite-size pieces to serve.

Chocho Nagaimo
Butterfly Chinese Yams   SERVES 4

⅓ *nagaimo* Chinese yam
1 hard boiled egg yolk
⅙oz (5g) dried bonito flakes
Stock (¾ cup (180ml) *dashi*, 1 teaspoon light soy sauce, ½ teaspoon *mirin*, 2½ teaspoons (10g) sugar and a pinch of salt)

1. Cut yam into ½" (1.5cm) wide slices and punch with butterfly-shaped die. Blanch them and plunge into water. Drain.

2. Combine the yams from step 2 with stock in a pan, cover the surface with the dried bonito flakes wrapped in cheese cloth and simmer until easily pierced with a skewer.

3. Roughly sieve the egg yolk to crumble

4. Cover the yams from step 2 with the crumbled egg yolk.

April *Futamono*   *Wakasa Guji Sakura-mushi*   P. 21
Steamed Wakasa Tilefish with   SERVES 4
Cherry Blossoms

About 5½oz (160g) Wakasa Tilefish fillets
8 *Warabi* bracken fern shoots (see below)
2.8oz (80g) *domyoji* flour
⅓oz (10g) salted cherry blossoms

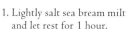

8 salted cherry tree leaves (soaked in water)
"A" Stock (½ cup (120ml) *dashi*, ½ teaspoon light soy sauce and a pinch of salt)
Gin-an thickened sauce; "B" stock (1¾ cups (400ml) *dashi*, 2 teaspoons light soy sauce and 0.4 teaspoon salt)
Kuzu dissolved in water
Ginger juice
Bubu arare tiny rice crackers

1. Remove the tilefish skin, sprinkle the fish with salt and let rest for a half day.

2. Towel dry the fish from step 1 and cut into 1⅓oz (40g) pieces and butterfly each, taking care not to cut all the way through.

3. Put domyoji in a bowl, add warmed stock "A" and roughly mix. Seal the bowl with plastic film and steam for about 10 minutes.

4. While the mixture from step 3 is still warm, chop the cherry blossoms and mix well. Make 1oz (30g) balls.

5. Wrap the balls from step 4 with the butterflied tilefish fillet, sandwich them between two cherry tree leaves, put in a container and steam for 7 to 8 minutes.

6. Prepare gin-an sauce: put the stock in sauce pan and heat, when it boils, thicken with kuzu dissolved in water.

7. Drain the balls from step 5 well, arrange with the warmed bracken and top with the sauce from step 6.

8. To serve, sprinkle with ginger juice and tiny crackers.

Warabi brackens

20 *warabi* bracken fern shoots
¼ teaspoon wood ashes
Stock for soaking (1½ cups (360ml) *dashi*, 2 teaspoons light soy sauce, ⅖ teaspoon (2g) salt and 1 teaspoon *mirin*)

1. Remove the hard end of stems. Rinse warabi and put in an earthenware pot and sprinkle with ash and mix well. Pour boiling water over them and cover, leave to cool.

2. When cool, change the water and soak them for about 30 minutes.

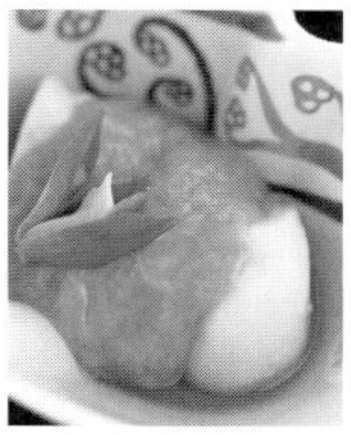

3. Blanch the shoots with boiling water and plunge them into cold water. Towel dry.

4. Bring the stock to a boil in a pan, add the bracken from step 3 and quickly take them out. When the stock is cool, steep the bracken fern shoots in it to absorb the flavor.

April *Su-zakana*   *Hotaru Ika to Sansai Tosa-zu-ae*   P. 22
Vinegared Firefly Squid and   SERVES 4
Wild Vegetables

12 firefly squids (tiny squid)
1 *yama udo* stalk

12 *kogomi*
½ *fuki*
Kinome leaf buds

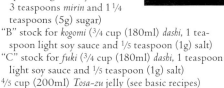

"A " stock for firefly squid (½ cup (120ml) sake, 2 teaspoons light soy, 2 teaspoons regular soy sauce, 3 teaspoons *mirin* and 1¼ teaspoons (5g) sugar)
"B" stock for *kogomi* (¾ cup (180ml) *dashi*, 1 teaspoon light soy sauce and ⅕ teaspoon (1g) salt)
"C" stock for *fuki* (¾ cup (180ml) *dashi*, 1 teaspoon light soy sauce and ⅕ teaspoon (1g) salt)
⅘ cup (200ml) *Tosa-zu* jelly (see basic recipes)

1. Rinse kogomi, and cut into 1" (3cm) lengths and soak in water with some ash. Blanch them with boiling water mixed with some ash. Take out and soak them in fresh water. Drain.

2. String fuki and cut into 1" (3cm) lengths. Blanch them and plunge into cold water. Drain.

3. Bring Stock "B" and "C" separately to a boil and take off the fire. Soak kogomi and fuki in their respective stocks.

4. Peel yama udo and cut into long pieces. Plunge them into salted water and drain.

5. Bring Stock "A" to a boil and cook firefly squid quickly and let cool.

6. Chop kinome leaf buds and add to Tosa-zu jelly from step 1 and combine well.

7. Dress the firefly squids, kogomi, fuki and yama udo with the tosa-zu jelly from step.

■ Spring *Mukozuke*
Madai   P. 24
Red Sea Bream

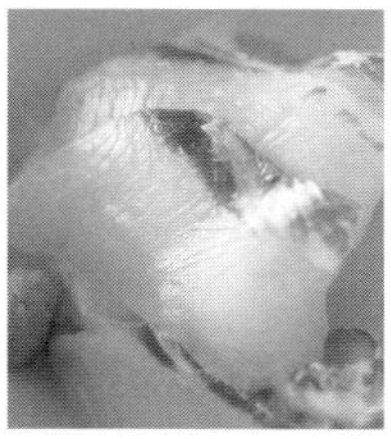

Madai red sea bream
Tosa-joyu (see basic recipes)
Grated *wasabi*

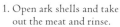

Fillet red sea bream, remove pin bones with tweezers and peel off the skin. Cut the fillet into thin slices and arrange on a plate. Serve with grated wasabi and Tosa soy sauce.

Akagai   P. 26
Ark Shells

Akagai ark shells
Tosa-joyu soy sauce (see basic recipes)
Grated *wasabi*

1. Open ark shells and take out the meat and rinse.

2. Sprinkle the ark shell meat with salt and rinse to remove any sliminess.

3. Cut crisscross diamond pattern into the ark shell meat.

4. Crush the akagai meat from step 3 with the broad side of a knife blade on a cutting board and when the muscle tightens arrange on a plate

5. Serve immediately with grated wasabi and Tosa soy sauce.

■ May *Hassun*
Tai Chimaki-zushi   P. 28

Sea Bream Sushi Wrapped in Bamboo Leaves

Sushi rice (see basic recipes)
4 Tablespoons sushi vinegar
 for raw sushi (see basic recipes)
Kinome leaf buds to taste
8oz (240g) of sea bream fillet
Pickling vinegar (see basic
 recipes)
Bamboo leaves

1. Prepare sushi rice. When cooled, add chopped kinome leaf buds.

2. Soak the sea bream fillet with its skin in pickling vinegar for about 30 minutes. Peel off the skin and cut into thin slices.

3. Take 1oz (30g) of the sushi rice from step 1 and make a sushi with a slice of the sea bream from step 2. Wrap the sushi in bamboo leaves in a cone shape, tie with silver and gold *mizuhiki* strings. Prepare the rest in the same way.

April *Yakimono* *Sakura Masu Ibushi-yaki*   P. 30

Smoked Cherry Salmon

1 *sakura masu* cherry salmon
 (2²/₃oz/80g×10 pieces)
Miso yuanji (see basic recipes)
A little sake (for rinsing)
2oz (50g) cherry tree wood chips
1 tablespoon sugar
kinome leaf buds as needed

1. Rinse cherry salmon, scale and fillet, remove pin bones with tweezers, remove skin and cut fillets into (80g) pieces.

2. Marinate the fillets from step 1 in miso yuanji for about 15 hours.

3. Rinse the trout in the water with a little sake and towel dry.

4. Skewer the trout from step 3 and broil over charcoal. Take off the skewers and quickly smoke in a smoker with the cherry wood chips mixed with sugar.

5. To serve, sprinkle with kinome leaf buds.

March *Takiawase* *Anago Toji-maki*   P. 33

Sea Eel and Yuba Rolls   SERVES 4

1 *anago* sea eel
4 sheets of *nama yuba* fresh soy-
 milk skin
"A" stock (1 ¹/₅ cups (280ml)
 dashi, 4 teaspoons light soy
 sauce and 4 teaspoons *mirin*)
4 *shiitake* mushrooms
"B" stock (³/₄ cup (180ml)
 dashi, 1 teaspoon light soy
 sauce and ¹/₅ teaspoon (1g) salt)
¹/₂ bunch of *hatakena*
"C" stock (³/₄ (180ml) *dashi*, 1 teaspoon light soy
 sauce and 1g salt)
Julienned *yuzu*

1. Blanch hatakena until brightened and plunge into cool water. Boil them in boiling stock "C" quickly and let cool on a rack. Bring the stock to a boil again and turn off the heat. When cooled, soak the hatakena in the stock for a half day.

2. Rinse sea eel, skewer and broil. Bone, cut into halves lengthwise and cut into 2" (4cm) wide slices (8 slices in total)

3. Spread a sheet of yuba and place two slices of the sea eel from step 2 on top and wrap in the yuba. Fasten the edges with a toothpick. Deep-fry and drain on a rack to remove excess oil.

4. Combine the Toji-maki from step 3 and "A" stock. Simmer with a drop lid until the rolls soak up the flavor of the stock.

5. Remove the stems of shiitake mushrooms and lightly singe over a flame to give them a toasty aroma. Simmer in "B" stock for 15 minutes.

6. Cut the hatakena from step 1 into serving pieces, warm them again and arrange with the toji maki from step 4 and the mushrooms from step 5. Top with julienned yuzu.

March *Yakimono* *Wakasa Guji Uni-yaki*   P. 34

Tilefish Grilled with Sea Urchin Roe

10×1 ¹/₃oz (40g) pieces of
 Wakasa tilefish
10.5 oz (300g) fresh sea
 urchin roe
2.2lb (1kg) *Saikyo miso* white
 miso paste
³/₄ cup (180ml) *nikiri zake*
 (sake from which the alcohol has been evaporated)
A pinch of salt

1. Dilute white miso with nikiri zake and mix well. Marinate the tilefish pieces in the mixture for about 13 hours.

2. Rinse the miso off the tilefish from step 2 with water mixed with some sake.

3. Skewer the tilefish skin side down and broil until cooked. Put sea urchin roe on top, sprinkle with salt and quickly sear the surface of sea urchin roe with a butane torch.

Simmered *fuki no to* with *miso*

10 *fuki no to*
1 cup (240m) *dashi*
1 Tablespoon (15g) *haccho miso* red miso paste
1 teaspoon (5g) *Saikyo miso* white miso paste

1. Deep-fry fuki no to and rinse with boiling water to remove excess oil.

2. Bring dashi to a boil and dissolve haccho miso and white miso and simmer the fuki no to until tender.

April *Yakimono* *Tofu Dengaku*   P. 36

Broiled Tofu with Miso Paste

1 block *kinugoshi* silken tofu
4 tablespoons leaf bud miso paste (see baked bamboo shoot recipe)
4 tablespoons white miso paste for broiled tofu (see
 below)
4 *kinome* leaf buds

1. Put weight on tofu to drain excess water. Cut into 8 serving pieces. Bake them in a 250°F (120°C) oven for about 15 minutes.

2. Spread each piece of tofu with miso paste and bake them in a 300°F (150°C) oven for 5 minutes.

3. Sear the surface of the miso with a propane torch and garnish the white miso dengaku with leaf bud miso paste and kinome buds.

Shiro dengaku miso
White miso paste for broiled tofu

10oz (300g) cooked miso paste (see *yaki takinoko*
 recipe)
7 Tablespoons (100ml) dashi
1 egg yolk

1. Add dashi and egg yolk to cooked miso paste and mix well.

2. Put the mixture in a pan on heat and taking care not to burn, cook for about 5 minutes stirring, let cool.

April *Gohan* *Takenoko-zushi*   P. 37

Bamboo Shoot Sushi

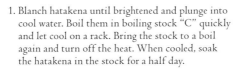

Sushi rice (see basic recipes)
3 to 4 Tablespoons sushi vinegar (see basic recipes)
4oz (120g) fresh bamboo
 shoots
¹/₃ piece of *abura age* deep-fried
 tofu
²/₃oz (20g) *chirimen jako* dried tiny fish
Tosa-zu flavored vinegar (see basic recipes)
¹/₆oz (5g) *kinome* leaf buds
Stock for bamboo shoots (7 Tablespoons (100ml)
 dashi, ¹/₂ tablespoon light soy sauce and ¹/₂ tablespoon *mirin*)

1. Cut bamboo shoots into small dice. Make cuts on side of abura age deep-fried tofu and turn inside out, then carefully remove the white part and use only the outer skin. Finely chop the skin into tiny pieces and rinse in boiling water to remove excess oil.

2. Simmer the bamboo shoots and the fried tofu from step 1 in stock until the bamboo shoots are easily pierced with a skewer.

3. Soak chirimen jako in Tosa-zu for 30 minutes.

4. Prepare sushi rice: combine the warmed and drained bamboo shoot mixture, drained jako with the sushi rice. When the sushi rice is cooled, add chopped kinome leaf buds.

5. Use the skin of bamboo shoots to hold the rice. Garnish with hajikami and ko no mono.

Hajikami Pickled ginger shoots

10 *hajikami* ginger shoots
Stock (10 Tablespoons water, 3 Tablespoons vinegar
 and 2 ¹/₂ tablespoons (30g) sugar)
A little salt and vinegar

1. Heat stock ingredients in a saucepan, taking care not to boil, to dissolve sugar. Let cool.

2. Peel hajikami ginger and cut into 2 1/2" (7cm) lengths.

3. Blanch the ginger from step 2 in boiling water with a little salt and vinegar and transfer to a sieve. Lightly salt and let cool. When cooled, soak the ginger in the stock from step 1, and leave until use.

Ko no mono

Kombu daikon and *nanohana*

In addition to the hajikami, there are two kinds of *ko no mono* pickles used to garnish the bamboo sushi. One is *kombu daikon*, a crisp salted pickle made from giant white radishes, Japanese chili peppers and kombu, and the other is made from *nanohana*, or rapini, a favorite spring vegetable. Chef Murata recommends using top quality Kyoto pickles if possible.

April *Yakimono* *Yaki Takenoko* P. 38

Baked Bamboo Shoots

1 bamboo shoot
A handful of *kome nuka* rice bran
Kinome leaf buds
Leaf bud miso paste (see below)

1. Cut off the top and cut the bamboo shoot in half lengthwise. Put the bamboo, rice bran, chili pepper in a pan and cover with cold water, top with a drop lid. Simmer until a bamboo skewer easily pierces the bottom and let cool. Rinse the rice bran off.

2. Bake them in a 350°F (180°C) oven for 15 minutes.

3. Cut the bamboo into quarters and cut with the tip of a knife to make it easy to eat with chopsticks. Sprinkle with chopped kinome leaf buds.

4. Serve with leaf bud miso paste. Soy sauce with Japanese mustard will fit as well.

Leaf bud *miso* paste

10oz (300g) cooked miso paste (see below)
1 2/3oz (50g) *kinome* leaf buds
1 1/3oz (40g) spinach (blanched and chopped finely)
Sansho Japanese pepper powder; to taste

1. Grind kinome leaf buds and spinach with a Japanese mortar and pestle. Add cooked miso paste and combine well. Sprinkle with sansho powder.

2. Strain

Cooked *miso* paste

1lb (500g) white miso paste
2 1/4 cups (540ml) sake

1. Add sake to white miso paste and mix well to dissolve miso. Put in a pan over heat and stir with a wooden spoon, taking care not to burn, simmer until the mixture returns to the original thickness of the white miso paste.

April *Shiizakana* *Waka-take-ni* P. 41

Wakame and Bamboo Shoots SERVES 4

1lb (400g) bamboo shoots (blanched)

"A" mixed stock (3 1/3 cups (800ml) *dashi*, 5 Tablespoons light soy sauce, a dash of salt and 3 Tablespoons *mirin*)
Dried bonito flakes

5 1/2oz (160g) *tai mako* sea bream ovaries
"B" mixed stock (2 cups (450ml) *dashi*, 1 Tablespoon light soy sauce, 1/2 Tablespoon *mirin* and 3/4 teaspoon sugar)
Dried bonito flakes

3oz (100g) *wakame* (salted wakame seaweed soaked in water)
Kinome leaf buds

1. Cut the bottom portion of the bamboo shoots into 3/4" (2cm) thick slices and make crisscross cuts on the pieces Cut the top portion of the bamboo shoots into semicircular pieces.

2. Put the bamboo shoots and "A" stock in a pan on heat, adding dried bonito flakes wrapped in gauze, cover with a drop lid, simmer for about 20 minutes on low heat.

3. Rinse and clean dark parts from the mako, cut into serving pieces and turn inside out. Drop the mako into boiling water and when they float to the top remove and plunge into ice water to cool. Drain well.

4. Combine the mako from step 3 and "B" stock and dried bonito flakes wrapped in gauze in a pan and simmer for about 20 minutes.

5. Take out the gauze wrapped bonito flakes, add wakame, and simmer for 1–2 minutes.

6. Arrange the bamboo shoots, wakame and sea bream ovaries in a bowl and pour the stock over them. Top with kinome leaf buds for garnish.

April *Tome-wan* *Ebi Shinjo Uguisu-jitate* P. 42

Pea Soup with Shrimp Balls

Deep-fried shrimp balls

3oz (100g) *shiba ebi* shrimp (shelled, deveined and rinsed)
1 tablespoon grated *yamaimo* mountain yams
1 1/3oz (40g) ground fish fillet
1 Tablespoon of kombu dashi
1/2 teaspoon dissolved *kuzu* (water: kuzu=1:1)
"A" stock (a pinch of salt, 1/2 teaspoon of light soy sauce, 1/5 teaspoon *mirin* and 1 teaspoon of egg white)
Black sesame seeds
Vegetable oil for frying

Pea soup

2 1/3oz (65g) fresh green peas, cooked in water with some baking soda, plunged into ice water, peeled and strained through a fine sieve)
"B" stock (13 1/2 fl.oz (400ml) *dashi*, 1 Tablespoon light soy sauce and 0.4 teaspoon salt)
Dissolved *kuzu* as needed

Petal-shaped *udo* (same recipe as April *hassun*)

1. Cut 1 2/3oz (50g) shrimp into 1/2" (1.5cm) pieces and coat with regular soy sauce.

2. Put the rest of the shrimp, ground fish meat, yams, kombu dashi powder, dissolved kuzu and "A" stock into a food processor and pulse to puree.

3. Combine the shrimp from step 1 and the mixture from step 2 in a bowl and shape into 1oz (30g) balls and sprinkle with black sesame seeds and deep-fry. Drain on a rack.

4. Puree the strained green peas in a food processor, dilute with some dashi.

5. Put "B" stock in a pan, bring to a boil, add the pea puree from step 4 and thicken with dissolved kuzu.

6. Place the shrimp balls in a serving bowl, cover with the soup and garnish with petal-shaped udo.

May *Futamono* *Wakasa Guji Shincha-mushi* P. 44

Steamed Tilefish SERVES 4
with Fresh Green Tea Leaves

1/2lb (250g) *guji* tilefish filet
1 1/2 beaten eggs
A pinch of salt
1 bunch *cha-soba* green tea noodles (dried ones)
Fresh *gyokuro* tea leaves as needed

Stock (1 1/2 cups (360ml) *dashi*, 1 teaspoon light soy sauce, 1 Tablespoon regular soy sauce and 4 teaspoons mirin)
Dried bonito flakes

Sliced green onions
Momiji oroshi grated daikon and chili peppers
Julienned nori

1. Remove the bones from tilefish fillet, peel off the skin and sprinkle with salt. Leave rest for a half day.

2. Mix the beaten eggs with a pinch of salt well, and fry them to make a very thin omelet like a crepe (larger than 8"×6" (20cm×15cm)).

3. Tie green tea noodles into a bundle and boil until still harder than *al dente*. Plunge them into water and drain well.

4. Cut the tile fishfrom step 1 into thin slices. Place the tilefish on top of a piece of plastic wrap. Cover the fish with the thin omelet from step 2 and the noodles from step 3. Sprinkle the gyokuro tea leaves along the center over the noodles. Using the plastic wrap make a roll with the noodles in the center.

5. Cleanly cut both ends and divide the roll into 4 pieces.

6. Place the roll from step 5 in a bowl and top with some gyokuro tea leaves. Cook in a steamer for 5–6 minutes.

7. Pour stock into a pan, boil and add gyokuro and dried bonito flakes, turn off heat and strain. Pour the soup over the roll from step 6. Garnish with momiji oroshii and sliced green onions.

Scattered Spring Sushi SERVES 4 TO 6

Sushi rice
"A" ingredients chopped and
mixed in sushi rice (about
30g each)
Simmered *anago* sea eel
Simmered dried *shiitake*
mushrooms
Koya-dofu dried tofu
Kanpyo dried shaved gourd

"B" ingredients scattered
over sushi rice
Momi nori dried seaweed
(toasted and crumbled)
Toasted white sesame seeds
Minced shrimp
Kinshi tamago thin ribbons of omelet

"C" ingredients final toppings
Simmered sea eels
Simmered shiitake mushrooms
Simmered *kuruma ebi* medium shrimps
Issun mame simmered broad beans
Warabi bracken fern shoots
Nanohana rapini
Blossom shaped ginger
Kinome leaf buds

1. Prepare each ingredient and sushi rice according
   to the following methods.

2. Combine "A" ingredients with cooked sushi rice.

3. Arrange the rice from step 2 and sprinkle with
   nori dried seaweed, sesame seeds, minced shrimps
   and eggs from "B" ingredients.

4. Arrange "C" ingredients atop step 3 rice.

Sushi rice (see basic recipe)

13oz (360g) dry rice
4 tablespoons sushi vinegar (see basic recipes)

1. Cook rice according to recipe on p. 162

2. Pour sushi vinegar over the rice and mix with a
   rice paddle using a slicing and tossing motion.
   The proper amount of sushi vinegar is 2 Tablespoons per $^3/_4$ cup (180ml) uncooked rice.

Simmered sea eels

2 filleted sea eels
Stock (1 cup (225ml) sake, 1 cup (225ml) water, $^1/_3$
cup (75ml) regular soy sauce, $^1/_3$ cup (75ml) *mirin*
and a little sugar)

1. Quickly blanch the filleted sea eels in boiling
   water to remove sliminess.

2. Bring stock in a pan to a boil, add sea eels and
   simmer for about 10 minutes.

3. When cooked, take the eels out of the stock and
   let cool.

4. Finely chop 1oz (30g) of the eel and cut the rest
   into about 1" (2.5cm) square pieces for topping.

Simmered *shiitake* mushrooms

$^2/_3$oz (20g) dried *shiitake* mushrooms
2 cups (500ml) water
Mixed stock (6$^3/_4$ fl.oz (200ml) stock from soaking
mushrooms, 6$^3/_4$ fl.oz (200ml) *dashi*, 2 Tablespoons sake, 4 teaspoons regular soy sauce, 2 teaspoons *mirin* and $^3/_4$ teaspoon sugar)

1. Clean dried shiitake mushrooms and soak in
   water for 24 hours. When they absorb the water,
   squeeze the mushrooms dry and remove hard ends
   of the stems.

2. Combine the mushrooms from step 1 and mixed
   stock in a pan and cover with a drop lid. Simmer
   on medium heat until the liquid is completely
   reduced.

3. When cooled cut off the stems. Finely chop 1oz
   (30g) of the mushrooms (including stems) for
   mixing with rice and cut remainder into thick
   slices for topping.

Simmered *Koya-dofu*

2 cubes 1oz (35g) *Koya-dofu* (freeze dried tofu)
Mixed stock (1 $^3/_4$ cups (400ml) *dashi*, 1 tablespoon
light soy sauce, 2 teaspoon *mirin*, 1 $^3/_4$ teaspoons
sugar and $^1/_3$ teaspoon salt)

1. Put Koya-dofu in a bowl, cover with cheesecloth
   and cover with 160°F (70°C) water. Leave for
   6–7 minutes and plunge the tofu into cold water.

2. Wash tofu in cool water 3–4 times, changing
   water and wringing dry each time. Drain well.

3. Heat tofu from step 2 with mixed stock in a sauce
   pan. Cover with a drop lid and when it boils, turn
   heat to low and simmer for about 12 minutes. Let
   the tofu steep in the stock until cool.

4. Drain and finely chop for mixing with rice.

Kanpyo

1 $^1/_3$oz (40g) *kanpyo* shaved gourd
Salt
Mixed stock (2 $^1/_2$ cups (600ml) *dashi*, 3$^3/_4$ Tablespoons (55ml) regular soy sauce, $^1/_2$ tablespoon
sugar and 4 teaspoons *mirin*)

1. Rinse kanpyo well, sprinkle with salt and rub.

2. After removing the salt, blanch in boiling salted
   water, plunge into cold water and drain.

3. Heat the well-drained kanpyo in a pan with mixed
   stock. When it boils, cover with a drop a lid and
   simmer on medium heat. After 7 minutes, remove
   the lid and cook until the liquid is completely
   reduced.

4. Chop finely to mix with rice.

Minced shrimp meat

3 $^1/_3$oz (100g) shrimp (shelled and deveined)
Stock (5 Tablespoons sake, 2 teaspoons light soy
sauce, 1 teaspoon *mirin*)

1. Finely chop shrimp.

2. Combine chopped shrimp from step 1 with stock,
   bring to a boil and simmer until all the liquid is
   reduced.

Kinshi tamago

2 eggs
pinch of salt

1. Beat eggs, strain and mix with salt.

2. Make two thin omelet sheets and slice into very
   fine ribbons.

Simmered *kuruma ebi*

4 medium shrimp
Mixed stock ($^1/_2$ cup (120ml) sake, 2 teaspoons
mirin and 2 teaspoons light soy sauce)

1. Remove the heads and devein the shrimp.

2. Bring mixed stock to a boil in a pan. Add the
   shrimps and simmer for about 2 minutes. Immediately cool the saucepan in a bowl of ice water.

3. When the shrimps have absorbed the flavor of the
   stock, cut into serving pieces.

Issun mame

8 fava bean pods
Mixed stock ($^3/_4$ cup (180ml) *dashi*, 1 teaspoon light
soy sauce, 1 teaspoon *mirin* and a pinch salt)

1. Shell bean pods and peel the beans.

2. Bring mixed stock to a boil in a small pan.
   Quickly blanch the beans from step 1 in the boiling stock, remove and cool them on a rack. Let
   the stock cool and when cooled return the beans
   to soak.

Warabi

20 *warabi* bracken fern shoots
$^1/_4$ teaspoon ash
Stock (1 $^1/_2$ cups (360ml) dashi, 2 teaspoons light
soy sauce, 0.4 teaspoon salt and 1 teaspoon *mirin*)

1. Cut off the hard part of stems. Rinse warabi, put
   into an earthenware pot, sprinkle with ash and
   mix roughly. Pour boiling water over them and
   cover the pot and leave to cool.

2. When cool, change the water and soak them in
   fresh water for about 30 minutes.

3. Blanch brackens in boiling water and then plunge
   them into cold water. Towel dry.

4. Bring the stock to a boil in a pan and add the
   brackens from step 3, quickly remove them.
   When the stock has cooled, put the warabi back
   in and let steep

5. Drain and cut into serving pieces.

Nanohana

12 *nanohana* rapini
Stock ($^1/_2$ cup+2 Tablespoons *dashi*, $^1/_2$ tablespoon
light soy sauce and a dash of salt)

1. Cut off the hard end of the stem, blanch rapini in
   salted water until bright green. Soak them in cold
   water and drain well.

2. Bring stock to a boil and turn off the heat. When
   cooled, soak the rapini from step 1 in it.

3. Drain and cut into serving pieces.

Blossom shaped ginger
Ginger
Sweetened rice vinegar (see basic recipes)

Cut ginger into a petal shapes and slice. Quickly
blanch in boiling water and soak in sweetened
vinegar.

Kusa Mochi   P. 49

Green Rice Cakes with
Red Bean Paste

SERVES 12

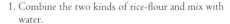

8 Tablespoons *shiratama-ko* rice-flour
8 Tablespoons *mochi-ko* rice-flour
³/4 cup (180ml) water
¹/2 cup (120ml) sugar
¹/2oz (15g) mugwort paste (see below)
1 cup (240g) sweet red bean paste
kinako toasted soybean power

1. Combine the two kinds of rice-flour and mix with water.
2. Spread a moist towel on a shallow tray. Pour the rice flour mixture on top, wrap in cheesecloth and cook in a steamer for 12-13 minutes.
3. Put the mixture from step 2 into a saucepan and add the half amount of sugar. Turn on the heat and mix well. Add the rest of sugar and mix again, then add the mugwort paste and mix well.
4. Divide sweet red bean paste into 12 portions and shape into balls.
5. Divide the mixture from step 3 and wrap the paste ball from step 4 in it. Dust with soybean powder to serve.

Mugwort paste

Blanch mugwort in boiling water with some ash and plunge into cold water. Drain well and puree in a food processor. If fresh mugwort is not available, dried mugwort powder can be used.

Annin-dofu   P. 49

Almond Jelly

SERVES 4

1¹/3 cup (320ml) milk
60g sugar
²/3oz (20g) *annin* powder Chinese apricot kernel powder
¹/3oz (10g) almond powder
1 teaspoon (5g) gelatin powder
A little Amaretto liqueur
Sugar syrup (¹/2 cup (125ml) water and 6 Tablespoons sugar)
Thai basil seeds

1. Lightly toast almond powder in a pan until a sweet aroma rises.
2. Combine annin powder and the almond powder from step 1 in a food processor, blend well.
3. Add some milk little by little to make a rough paste.
4. Mix the rest of milk, sugar, gelatin powder and the paste from step 3 and pour into a saucepan. Let the gelatin soak for a while.
5. Heat and stir to mix well and dissolve the gelatin. Use a thermometer and heat to 176°F (80°C)
6. Let cool and strain through cheese cloth. Add Amaretto and refrigerate in a rectangular pan.
7. Make syrup and refrigerate. Soak basil seeds in water.

8. Cut the tofu from step 6 into serving pieces and place in a bowl with basil seeds. Cover with the syrup.

SUMMER

Hamo-zushi   P. 52

Hamo Sushi

SERVES 10

14oz (400g) *hamo*
2 tablespoons grilling sauce (see below)
1lb (420g) steamed sushi rice, 1 cup (210g) uncooked (see basic recipes)
Sansho (Japanese ground pepper) to taste

1. Rinse the hamo and then fillet it, removing the backbone, fin, and belly bones. Slice through pin bones with a heavy knife making cuts perpendicular to the length (see page 68.) Skewer the filets across their length. Grill the fillets over hot coals. Brush with the grilling sauce and grill again until dry. Repeat the grilling process.
2. Divide the sushi rice and shape into two sticks the same length as the hamo fillet.
3. Put one piece of grilled hamo skin-side up on a clean, slightly moist tea towel and sprinkle with sansho pepper, then cover the fillet with one stick of sushi rice. Roll in the towel to shape and compress gently to create a half round stick-like piece.
4. Repeat the process with the other fillet. Cut each into 10 pieces.

For grill sauce

Hamo scraps including bones, and liver.
1¹/4 cups (300ml) regular soy sauce
1¹/4 cups (300ml) *sake*
1¹/4 cups (300ml) *mirin*

1. Cut the scraps into medium pieces and grill them until lightly browned.
2. Combine browned scraps from step 1 in a pan with all other sauce ingredients, cook over low heat until the stock is reduced by ¹/3 and filter.

Kawa Ebi

River Shrimp

20 kawa ebi, small freshwater shrimp

For stock
⁴/5 cup (200ml) sake
1 tablespoon light soy sauce
2 teaspoon *mirin*

1. Remove shrimp legs and antennae and trim tails into a v-shape.
2. Combine the sake, light soy sauce and mirin in a pan, bring to a boil then add shrimp.
3. When cooked, remove shrimp and let cool for 3 to 4 minutes. Reserve stock and let cool. When stock is cooled, add shrimp and let them macerate.

Bekko Shoga

Amber Ginger

2 hands of young ginger
¹/2 dried Japanese chili pepper
⁴/5 cup (160g) sugar
1 cup (240ml) water

1. Scrape the skin off the ginger and cut ginger into ¹/3" (8mm) pieces. Boil ginger pieces with the chili pepper and drain, let soak in fresh water. Repeat the boiling and soaking several times to mellow the flavor.
2. Drain the ginger, cook in a steamer for 10 minutes. Remove and let the ginger dry well.
3. Caramelize the sugar in a heavy pan. Add 1 cup water and ginger and simmer for about 30 minutes.

Wakasa Guji Kyuri-maki

Tilefish Roll with Cucumber

4¹/4oz (120g) tilefish (one side fillet)
1¹/2 Japanese cucumbers
2oz (60g) ginger
¹/2 cup (120ml) sweetened vinegar (see basic recipes)
Tosa-su flavored vinegar (see basic recipes)

1. Salt tilefish fillet, refrigerate for 2 to 3 hours.
2. Peel the cucumbers in a single continuous sheet using *katsura-muki* technique (*see glossary*) and soak them in a two percent solution of saltwater.
3. Peel ginger and cut into fine julienne. Blanch in boiling water and drain. Soak julienned ginger in sweetened vinegar.
4. Soak the tilefish fillet from step 1 in Tosa-zu for 5 minutes. Then, slice thinly and place on cucumber from step 2. Use the ginger from step 3 as a core and roll the cucumber and tilefish into a cylinder. Slice into ¹/3" (7mm) rounds.

Tako no Ko

Octopus Roe

7oz (200g) octopus roe (small)
Stock (2 cups (500ml) *dashi*, 2 teaspoons light soy sauce, 1 tablespoon *mirin*, ²/5 cup (100ml) sake), 1 teaspoon sugar, ¹/2 tablespoon salt)
¹/5oz (5g) dried bonito flakes

1. Tear the octopus roe sacs and turn inside out. Parboil and remove when they float to the surface. Plunge into cold water, let rest for a while and drain.
2. Combine ingredients for the stock, bring to a boil and add the roe from step 1. Top with a drop lid made of bonito flakes wrapped in cheese cloth, simmer for about 30 minutes to infuse the eggs with flavor.

Rikyu-fu to Aouri Kaminari-boshi Hisui-ae

Rikyu-fu and Salted Green Gourd

3oz (100g) seeded cucumber
¹/2 *Rikyu-fu* (wheat gluten)
Stock (³/4 cup (180ml) *dashi*, 2 teaspoons light soy sauce, 1 teaspoon *mirin*)

3 1/3oz (100g) *aoura* green gourd
3 tablespoons *Tosa-zu* jelly (see basic recipes)

Light soy sauce
Ginger juice

1. To prepare green gourd, cut off the top and bottom and punch the core out with a circular mold. Beginning at the bottom make a cut about 1/3" (7mm) thick and continue in a spiral fashion to make a long spring shape. Soak in 2% solution of saltwater for an hour and drain. Let it dry in a shady, well ventilated place for 12 hours. Cut the dried gourd "spring" into pieces about 1 1/4" (3cm) long.

2. Cook the fu in boiling water for a minute and drain. Combine fu, and stock ingredients in a pan and simmer for about 5 minutes. Let the fu rest in the stock for a while, then drain and cut the fu into 1 1/4" (3cm) pieces.

3. Grate the cucumber and squeeze out excess liquid.

4. Combine the grated cucumbers from step 3 with Tosa-zu jelly and adjust the taste with light soy sauce and ginger juice. Add the gourd from step 1 and Rikyu-fu from step 2 and mix well.

Hajikami

Pickled ginger Shoots

See p. 165

June *Sakizuke*　*Aoume Shiro-wine-ni*　P. 54

Green Japanese Plums in White Wine　SERVES 4

8 *ao ume* fresh green Japanese
　plums
For syrup
1 1/2 cups (360ml) water
4 Tablespoons (50g) sugar
For white wine syrup
3/4 cup (180ml) white wine
3/4 cup (180ml) water
1/2 cup (100g) sugar

1. Prick the entire surface of the ume plums with a bamboo skewer or toothpick, and soak in a 10% solution of saltwater overnight.

2. Put plums into a copper pot and cover with water, Heat to almost boiling and drain. Repeat several times to remove sourness.

3. Combine the simmered plums with the syrup ingredients in a sauce pan, and cover with a cooking-paper drop lid. Simmer on low heat for about 20 to 30 minutes, let cool.

4. Bring the white wine syrup to a boil in a saucepan, turn off heat and let cool.

5. Remove plums from step 3 syrup and transfer them into the wine syrup pot. Cook for about 30 minutes taking care to not to let syrup boil, turn off heat, cool, and refrigerate.

August *Sakizuke*　*Ichijiku Saikyou-ni*　P. 56

Figs Simmered in White Miso　SERVES 4

4 figs

---

1 3/4 cups (400ml) water
2.8oz (80g) *Saikyo* miso
　white miso paste (choose
　one that is not too sweet)
1/3oz (10g) *katsuo bushi* (dried
　bonito flakes)

Fig sauce

4 Tablespoons (60ml) fig cooking liquid
1oz (25g) *kuzu* or corn starch dissolved in just less
　than 10 teaspoons water
Japanese mustard powder (or Coleman's mustard
　powder) to taste
Ito hana katsuo (threads of dried bonito)

1. Blanch the figs quickly in boiling water to loosen skins. Cool under running water, peel and drain.

2. Dissolve the Saikyo miso in water and bring to a boil. Add figs from step 1 and cook on low heat for 20 to 30 minutes, covered with dried bonito flakes wrapped in gauze. Let figs cool in the stock, refrigerate.

3. Make the fig sauce: bring 3/4 cup+1 tablespoon (200ml) of fig cooking liquid to a boil. Thicken with the kuzu mixture. Let cool and combine with prepared Japanese mustard to taste.

4. Place the chilled figs on a plate, top with sauce from step 3 and garnish with ito hana katsuo.

July *Naka-choko*　**Tomato** *Suri-nagashi*　P. 56

Chilled Tomato Soup　SERVES 4 TO 6

"A" For fresh tomato puree
10oz (300g) large ripe
　tomatoes (*Yubi*)
5oz (150g) cherry tomatoes
　(*Kyo Temari*)

"B" For tomato reduction
14oz (400g) large ripe
　tomatoes (*Yubi*)
7oz (200g) cherry tomatoes
　(*Kyo Temari*)
A little salt
A little lemon juice

"C" For creamy *yuba* (soy-milk skin) topping
10oz (300g) *kumiage yuba* (a rich soy-milk skin)
1/2oz (60ml) *dashi*
1/8 teaspoon sesame paste
Pinch of salt
1/2 teaspoon light soy sauce
Garnishes
Japanese cucumbers
Chives
Shiso buds

1. Chop "A" tomatoes and puree in a food processor, strain through a fine sieve, reserve.

2. Chop "B" tomatoes, puree and strain them through a fine sieve. Simmer them in a non-reactive pot until reduced to about 7 Tablespoons (100ml) and let cool.

3. When cool, combine the tomato puree from step 1 and the reduction from step 2, adjust the taste with salt and lemon juice. Refrigerate to chill well.

4. Put the "C" ingredients in a food processor, puree, refrigerate to chill well.

To serve

Divide tomato soup from step 3 among 4 to 6 chilled bowls and gently top with yuba cream mixture, garnish with peeled and roughly chopped cucumbers, chopped chives and shiso buds.

July *Hiyashi-bachi*　*Natsuyasai Takiawase*　P. 58

Chilled Summer Vegetables　SERVES 4

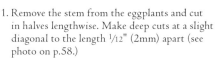

Eggplant, winter melon,
　pumpkin, lotus root,
　Tanaka chili peppers

Eggplant

2 Japanese eggplants
"A" Stock (1 3/4 cups
　(400ml) *dashi*, 1 table-
　spoon light soy sauce, 1/3
　teaspoon salt, and 1 tea-
　spoon sugar
1/4oz (8g) *katsuo bushi* (Shaved bonito)

1. Remove the stem from the eggplants and cut in halves lengthwise. Make deep cuts at a slight diagonal to the length 1/12" (2mm) apart (see photo on p.58.)

2. Bring "A" stock to a boil and drop in eggplants. Cover with a drop lid made from the dried bonito flakes wrapped in cheese cloth and cook for 5 to 6 minutes.

3. To preserve color, plunge into ice water immediately.

Winter melon

4 pieces winter melon 1 1/5" (3cm) square (about 1oz/30g each)

"B" stock (1 1/4 cups (300ml) *dashi*, 1 tablespoon light soy sauce, pinch of salt and tablespoon *mirin*)

1/4oz (8g) dried bonito flakes

1. Peel winter melon. Rub the surface with salt, boil in salted water for about 15 minutes. Plunge into ice water to cool and drain.

2. Bring "B" stock to a boil and drop in the winter melon. When it boils again, cover with drop lid made from dried bonito flakes wrapped in cheese cloth and simmer for about 5 minutes. Plunge into ice water to cool and drain. Reserve stock for gelatin.

Chrysanthemum pumpkin

4 pieces of pumpkin about 1 1/2oz each (45g)
"C" stock (4/5 cup (200ml) *dashi*, 2 teaspoons light soy sauce, 1/2 teaspoon salt, 1 tablespoon sugar)

1. Cut the pumpkin pieces into chrysanthemum shapes (see picture p.59.) Pare the corners of the pumpkin pieces and peel the skin in a striped pattern.

2. Put pumpkin pieces in cold water and bring to a boil, lower heat and simmer briefly, remove from water.

3. Cook pumpkin in "C" stock over low heat for 5 to 6 minutes taking care not to destroy its shape. Let cool in stock.

Young lotus root

2oz (60g) young lotus root (cut into a flower-shape
²/₅"/1cm thickness)
"D" stock (⁴/₅ cups (200ml) *dashi*, 1 teaspoon light
soy sauce, 1 teaspoon *mirin* and a little salt

1. Blanch the lotus root in boiling water with a little
   vinegar and remove.
2. Bring "D" stock in a pan to a boil. Drop in the
   lotus roots from step 1 and cook for 7 to 8 minutes. Let cool.

Gobo **root**

2⁴/₅oz (80g) young *gobo* root (rinsed, skin scraped
off and cut into pieces 1¹/₂"/4cm long)
"E" stock (10 Tablespoons *dashi*, 1 teaspoon light
soy sauce and ¹/₂ teaspoon *mirin*)

Blanch the gobo in boiling water with vinegar,
remove and simmer in "E" stock for 7 to 8 minutes, turn off heat and let cool in the stock.

Tanaka chili pepper

8 Tanaka chili peppers
"F" stock (³/₄ cup (180ml) *dashi*, 2 teaspoons light
soy sauce and 1 teaspoon *mirin*)

1. De-stem the chili peppers. Skewer the peppers
   and broil. Plunge into ice water.
2. Bring "F" stock to a boil. Quickly simmer the
   peppers from step 1, remove and fan to cool,
   reserve stock.
3. When stock is cooled, soak peppers in it.

Final assembly

1²/₃ cup (400ml) of the reserved winter melon "B"
stock
¹/₁₀oz (3g) gelatin

1. Bring the reserved liquid to a boil, add the gelatin,
   and stir to dissolve. Strain and cool.
2. Arrange chilled vegetables on a plate. When stock
   from step 1 is slightly thickened but still liquid,
   pour the over the surface of the vegetables. Chill
   until set. Garnish with fine julienne of green yuzu
   skin.

July *Futamono* **Buta Kaku-ni**   P. 61

Simmered Pork Cubes   SERVES 10

3.3lbs (1.5Kg) pork belly cut in 2" (5cm) cubes

"A" 2¹/₄ cups (540ml) sake
2¹/₄ cups (540ml) water
2¹/₂oz (70g) black sugar
2 tablespoons regular soy
  sauce
2¹/₂oz (70g) *haccho miso*

"B" 10.5oz (300g) peeled
  potatoes
1³/₄ cups (400ml) *dashi*
1 tablespoon light soy sauce
A little *mirin*
3 tablespoons of *kuzu* slurry thickener (water 7
  Tablespoons/100ml: kuzu 1²/₃oz/50g)
"C" 10 pieces of winter melon 1.5" long×1.2"×1"
  (3.5cm×3cm×2.5cm)

Stock (2¹/₂ cups (600ml) *dashi*, 2 tablespoons light
  soy sauce, pinch of salt and 2 Tablespoons *mirin*)

0.35oz (10g) dried bonito flakes
"D" 12 green beans
¹/₃ cup (80ml) *dashi*
1 teaspoon light soy sauce
A pinch salt
Prepared Japanese mustard

To make simmered pork

1. Sear all sides of meat chunks in a frying pan, then
   simmer on very low heat in a pot of rice rinse
   water for 15 to 16 hours.
2. Rinse the meat in cool water, and then put meat
   in a pot, cover with cold water and bring to a boil.
   Drain, steam for 10 minutes.
3. Combine the "A" sake, water, black sugar and
   regular soy sauce in a pan and dissolve the haccho
   miso. Add the pork from step 2 and cook for 30 to
   40 minutes until the pork absorbs the flavor.

Potatoes

1. Thinly slice the potatoes. Cook in a steamer until
   soft, push them through a fine sieve.
2. Bring the "B" dashi, light soy sauce and mirin to a
   boil. Add the kuzu slurry to thicken. Let cool.
3. Put the step 1 and 2 products in a food processor
   and pulse to blend well.

Winter melon

1. Peel winter melon pieces. Rub the surface with
   salt, boil it in salted water for about 15 minutes.
   Remove to a bowl of cold water, when cooled,
   drain.
2. Bring the "C" stock to a boil and add the step 1
   winter melon. When the stock returns to a boil,
   top with a drop lid made from the dried bonito
   flakes covered in cheese cloth and simmer on low
   heat for about 5 minutes. Turn off heat and let
   cool as melon absorbs the flavor of the stock.

Green beans

1. De-stem the green beans, string, and cut them
   into 1¹/₃" (3.5cm) long pieces.
2. Blanch the green beans in boiling salted water,
   plunge into ice water.
3. Bring the "D" ingredients to a boil and quickly
   cook the beans from step 2, remove and plunge
   into ice water. Return stock to a boil, turn off
   heat and let cool. When stock is cool add the
   green beans and let them absorb the flavor.

To serve

Warm up each of the ingredients and the plate.
Arrange the pork and winter melon and pour the
potato puree over them. Garnish with the green
beans and prepared Japanese mustard.

July *Sakizuke* **Nama Uni-dofu**   P. 62

Fresh Sea Urchin Tofu

FOR AN 8.5"/21CM SQUARE CONTAINER

10 oz (300g) fresh sea urchin roe
3⁴/₅ cups (900ml) soy milk (unsweetened)
0.07 oz (2g) *kanten* seaweed gelatin
¹/₂ teaspoon (2g) gelatin power

1¹/₄ cups (300 ml) *dashi*
¹/₅ oz (6g) *nigari* magnesium
salts, the traditional tofu
makers' coagulant

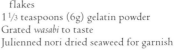

Kuidashi **jelly**

1¹/₂ cups (350ml) *dashi*
¹/₅ cup (50ml) light soy
  sauce
¹/₅ cup (50ml) *mirin*
¹/₆ oz (5g) dried bonito
  flakes
1¹/₃ teaspoons (6g) gelatin powder
Grated *wasabi* to taste
Julienned nori dried seaweed for garnish

1. Strain 2 oz (60g) fresh sea urchin roe through a
   fine sieve and combine with soy milk.
2. Tear kanten into small pieces and soften in water.
   Drain well.
3. Combine dashi and gelatin powder with the
   kanten from step 2 in a pan, bring to a boil and
   cook until the liquid is reduced by ¹/₃ while stirring occasionally, let cool slightly.
4. Heat the soy milk from step 1. When it is
   warmed, add the mixture from step 2 and cook,
   stirring with a wooden paddle taking care not to
   burn, until the temperature reaches 158°F–167°F
   (70°C–75°C) (if it hits 175°F/80°C it won't
   harden).
5. Add nigari in the mixture from step 4, mix once
   with a paddle and immediately pour the mixture
   into a container.
6. When the surface starts to harden, quickly scatter
   the rest of fresh sea urchin roe over the surface.
   Seal with a glass plate to make the surface flat and
   smooth. Refrigerate.
7. When hardened, cut the tofu into serving pieces,
   cover with kuidashi jelly (see below) and garnish it
   with julienned nori dried seaweed.

Kuidashi **jelly**

1. Bring dashi, light soy sauce and mirin to a boil.
   Add dried bonito flakes, remove from heat and let
   cool, strain.
2. Add gelatin powder in the cooled stock from step
   1 and cook constantly mixing to dissolve the gelatin, when it is dissolved, turn off heat and let cool.
3. Put the mixture from step 2 in a refrigerator to
   harden and then put it go through a fine sieve.
4. Add grated wasabi to the jelly from step

■ Summer *Mukozuke*

Kuruma Ebi   P. 64

Shrimp

1. Blanch shrimps in boiling water with a dash
   of salt for two seconds
   to brighten their color.
   Immediately plunge them
   into ice water.
2. Remove the head, shell
   and devein, slicing down
   the back.
3. Drop the shrimps from

step 2 in ice water again. Towel dry and cut into serving pieces.

4. Serve with grated wasabi and Tosa soy sauce see basic recipes.

Shima Aji   P. 64

Yellow Jack

1. Rinse yellow jack and fillet it, remove pin bones with tweezers. Peel off the skin and cut into thin slices.

2. Serve with Tosa soy sauce (see basic recipes) and grated wasabi.

July *Mukozuke* *Hamo Otoshi*   P. 68

Blanched *Hamo*

1lb (400–500g) *hamo*

1. Rinse the hamo and fillet it. Remove the backbone, fin and belly bones and after slicing the pin bones (*see page 68*) cut it into bite-size pieces.

2. Bring a one percent solution of saltwater to a boil and place the pieces of hamo skin-side down on a flat strainer with a long handle. Lower only as far as the skin into the boiling water for 15 seconds, then quickly lower the whole pieces. Immediately remove and plunge the hamo pieces into ice water.

3. When the hamo pieces from step 2 are cool, take them out of the ice water and drain well.

Ume sauce

3¹/₃oz (100g) ume (Japanese plum) paste
2 teaspoon regular soy sauce
7 Tablespoons (100ml) sake
1 teaspoon *mirin*
Dried bonito flakes

1. Combine soy sauce, sake and mirin in a saucepan and bring to a boil. Add bonito flakes, turn off heat and let cool.

2. When cooled, filter sauce through cheese cloth and mix well with ume paste.

August *Shiizakana* *Hamo Nabe*   P. 71

Hamo Hot Pot   SERVES 4

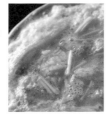

7–9oz (200–250g) *hamo* fillet with pin bones cut
Mitsuba (trefoil) (stalks only)
6 Japanese eggplants
"A" Stock (3¹/₂ cups (600ml) *dashi*, 3 tablespoons+1 teaspoon light soy sauce and 3 tablespoons+1 teaspoon *mirin*)
"B" Stock (4 tablespoons *dashi*, a little light soy sauce)

Topping

4 eggs
Sansho ground Japanese pepper

1. Prepare hamo fillet by slicing through tiny bones (see page 68) then cut the fillets into bite-size pieces.

2. Cut mitsuba stalks into ³/₄" (1.5cm) pieces.

3. Punch holes in the eggplants with a chopstick opposite the stem end. Broil on high heat until the skins are charred. Peel them and dice into ³/₄" (1.5cm) cubes.

4. Bring "A" stock a boil and simmer the hamo from step 1. Turn off flame and let fish cool in the stock. When cool, drain the stock, reserve.

5. Combine ¹/₂ cup (120ml) stock from step 4 and "B" dashi, adjust the taste with light soy sauce.

6. Place the broiled eggplant in a shallow fry pan, top with hamo and cover with the *dashi* from step 5. Put on medium flame. When the *dashi* boils, pour in ²/₃ beaten eggs and mix quickly, scatter *mitsuba* stems and then pour on the rest of the eggs, cook until eggs are just set. Sprinkle with *sansho* before serving.

August *Sakizuke* *Kohaku Kan*   P. 72

Hamo in Amber

SERVES 10, ONE 5"(12CM)×6" (15CM)×2"(5CM) PAN
"A" 3¹/₃oz (100gms) *hamo* roe
Stock (4 tablespoons sake, 4 tablespoons water, ¹/₂ teaspoon light soy sauce and ¹/₂ teaspoon *mirin*)
"B" 1oz (30g) *hamo* liver
¹/₂oz (15g) *hamo* swim bladder
Stock (3 tablespoons+1 teaspoon sake, 3 tablespoons+1 teaspoon water and 1 teaspoon regular soy sauce)
¹/₂ teaspoon sugar
"C" 6oz (175g) *hamo* filet (rinsed and filleted then sliced across the bones (see text on page 68) cut into pieces about 10g each
Stock (Slightly less than 1 cup (225ml) *dashi*, 5 tablespoons sake, 2 teaspoons light soy sauce, 4 teaspoons regular soy sauce and 2 tablespoons *mirin*)
"D" 8–9 pieces of okra
Stock (³/₄ cup (180ml) *dashi*, 1 teaspoon light soy sauce and a little salt)
"E" stock (1 cup (250ml) *dashi*, a little ginger juice and a little light soy sauce)
³/₄ Tablespoon (10g) gelatin powder
"F" *kuidashi*
Stock (1¹/₄ cup (300ml) *dashi*, 5 teaspoons light soy sauce, 5 teaspoons mirin and ¹/₄oz (7.5g) dried bonito flakes)
"G" garnishes
Jyakago lotus roots
2.8oz (80g) lotus roots
³/₄ cup+1 Tablespoon (200ml) *dashi*
1 teaspoon light soy sauce
1 teaspoon *mirin*
a little salt
green *yuzu*
shiso buds

For jelly

1. Rinse the hamo roe well under running water, remove veins and membrane

2. Combine roe with "A" stock and simmer until the liquid is almost completely reduced, taking care not to burn.

3. Rinse the hamo liver and swim bladder and blanch in boiling water, remove and soak in cool water.

4. Remove swim bladder from water and slice finely perpendicular to its length.

5. Combine the liver and swim bladder with "B" stock and simmer. When cool, cut the liver into small pieces.

6. Simmer prepared hamo fillet pieces in "C" stock.

7. Rub okra with salt to remove tiny hairs. Cut off the tops and tips and remove the seeds using a bamboo skewer. Cut them into ¹/₈" (2–3mm) thick rounds.

8. Blanch the okra in salted water, cool under running water, drain.

9. Bring "D" stock to a boil and let cool. Soak okra in cooled stock.

10. Filter cooled "D" stock and add hot "E" stock

11. Dissolve powdered gelatin in the stock from step 10, let cool until it gels slightly, spoon ¹/₄ of the jellied stock to a bowl and fold in the prepared hamo roe, pour into a 5"×6"×2" container (12.5cm×15cm×5cm). Top with hamo meat, chopped liver and swim bladder and cover with half of the jelly. Top with okra and the remainder of the jelly, refrigerate.

Kuidashi

1. Combine "F" liquid ingredients in a pot, bring to boil, put in the dried bonito flakes, turn off flame, let cool and filter.

To make *jyakago* lotus root

1. Cut the lotus root into a jyakago-shape (see photo on p.73). Blanch in boiling water with a little vinegar, drain. Simmer in the "F" stock.

To serve

1. When the jelly is hardened, cut into serving pieces with a sharp knife.

2. Place a bamboo ring on a plate and top with a lotus leaf. Arrange the cut jelly, jyakago lotus root on the leaf and sprinkle with kuidashi. Garnish with the grated skin of green yuzu and shiso buds.

June *Yakimono* *Ayu Shio-yaki*   P. 74

Grilled Ayu   SERVES 4

8 small *ayu* (a fresh water fish, see page 74)
Iri shio (toasted sea salt)

For *tade* paste

7oz (200g) *tade no ha* (water pepper leaves)
1¹/₃oz (40g) *Umi no Sei* (sea salt)

For *Yaki-zu* (vinegar for grilling)

0.35oz (10g) *kombu*, kelp

3 cups (750ml) water
2 1/4 cups (530ml) rice vinegar
1 teaspoon (5g) salt

1. To make tade paste, puree tade (water pepper) leaves and sea salt in food processor.

2. For yaki-zu grilling vinegar: soak kelp in water and vinegar until softened. Put in sauce pan, add salt, heat until almost boiling, turn off flame, let cool, remove kelp.

3. For tade-zu (water pepper vinegar): Dissolve 1/3 teaspoon tade paste in 1 tablespoon yaki-su from step 2.

4. For grilled ayu: Thread individual fish onto skewers, sprinkle toasted salt all over fish. Grill over hot coals until their skin becomes crisp.

Serve with tade-zu.

August Yakimono *Awabi Iso-yaki* P. 76

Abalone in a Salt Dome SERVES 4

4 small abalones in shell
17.5oz (500g) *uni* fresh sea urchin roe
1oz (30g) *daikon* giant radish
Stock (6 3/4 cups (1.6l) sake, 3 2/5 cups (800ml) water, a little sugar and a little light soy sauce)
2.2lbs (1kilo) salted *wakame* (an edible seaweed)
Garnish
4 *sudachi* citrus

1. Separate the abalone meat from the shell and scrub with a brush. Remove the frilly black edge with a sharp knife.

2. Combine the abalone and daikon cut into 1"(2.5cm) rounds and bring to a boil, turn down heat and simmer, then remove daikon when abalone is tender. Add sugar and then, after a bit, light soy sauce. Cook until the stock is reduced (about 2 to 3 hours).

3. Remove abalone from the pan. Separate the liver from the meat (reserve for the liver sauce) and cut the meat into 1/2" (1.25cm) thick slices.

4. Rinse the wakame well to remove the salt, arrange half of it under the abalone shells. Place abalone in the shell and put sea urchin roe between the slices. Cover with the rest of the wakame and seal the top with aluminum foil.

Salt Dome

4.4lbs (2kilo) salt
1 egg white
A little water

1. In a bowl, work the salt with the egg white and a little water to make a soft paste. Mound over the foil covered abalone and bake in a 320°F degree oven (160°C) for 20 minutes.

Liver sauce

1 1/2oz (45g) strained abalone liver
2 1/2 tablespoons sake
1/2 tablespoons *tsukuri-shoyu* (strong soy sauce for sashimi)
1 tablespoon *sudachi* juice

---

1. Put the cooked abalone liver through a fine sieve and then work it in a *suribachi* with a *surikogi* (Japanese mortar and pestle) while adding the liquid ingredients to make a sauce.

To Serve

Remove the salt dome without breaking it and peel off the aluminum foil, remove wakame from top. Place the shell on a plate and cover again with the baked salt dome. Garnish with the liver sauce and a half sudachi.

June Futamono *Anago Hirosu* P. 78

Sea Eel Tofu Balls SERVES 10

For *Hirosu*

2 filleted *anago* (sea eels)
"A" stock (3/5 cup (150ml) sake 3/5 cup (150ml) water, 3 tablespoons regular soy sauce, 3 tablespoons *mirin*, and a little sugar)

1 2/3oz (50g) carrots
1 1/3oz (40g) *kikurage* cloud ear mushrooms soaked in water to soften
2 1/2oz (75g) *yurine* lily bulbs
1/2oz (15g) toasted and ground sesame seeds
1/2 egg yolk
1 2/3oz (50g) *kumiage yuba* fresh soy-milk skin
1 1/2 teaspoons *goma abura* toasted sesame seed oil
7oz (200g) *shibori-dofu* well drained *momen* tofu
3 1/3oz (100g) *tsukushi imo*, tsukushi yam
2 tablespoons fresh cream
A little milk
1/2 teaspoon light soy sauce
A little sea salt
Some white poppy seeds
Vegetable oil for deep-flying
"B" stock (4/5 cup (200ml) niban-dashi, 1 teaspoon light soy sauce and a pinch of salt.)

For *kinome an sansho* pepper leaf sauce

Kinome Japanese pepperleaf buds
"C" stock (1qt (1L) *dashi*, 5 teaspoons (25ml) light soy sauce, 1tsp *mirin*, 1 teaspoon (5g) salt)
Kuzu starch dissolved in water (kuzu 1 2/3oz/50g: water 6 3/4 Tablespoons)

For garnish

15 Green beans, par boil, cut into half lengthways and remove seeds.

1. Dice the carrot into 1/8" (3mm)-cubes. Soak the cloud ear mushrooms in water and chop into bite-size pieces. Clean the lily bulb and dice into 3/8" (1cm)-cubes.

2. Simmer the carrot and the cloud ear mushroom in 4/5 cup (200ml) dashi, combined with 1 teaspoon light soy sauce and a pinch of salt. Steam the lily bulb pieces for about 5 minutes and lightly salt.

3. Simmer anago in "A" stock and cut into 3/4" (2cm)-square pieces.

4. Pulse toasted and ground sesame seeds, egg yolk, kumiage yuba, and sesame seed oil in a food processor and put into a bowl.

5. Puree well drained tofu in a food processor, add peeled and grated tsukushi yam and the paste from step 4. Mix well and adjust the thickness

---

of the mixture by adding fresh cream and a little milk (no more than 3 tablespoons). Adjust seasoning with light soy sauce and salt.

6. Transfer the paste to a bowl, fold in the carrot and the cloud ear mushrooms and divide into 10 portions. Put some sea eel and some lily bulb into each one and roll into a ball shape. Sprinkle with poppy seeds.

7. Deep fry the hirosu balls until golden, remove let cool and then pour boiling water over them to remove oil. Simmer in "B" stock.

8. To make the kinome sauce, bring "C" stock to a boil, thicken with kuzu powder dissolved in water, adding a little at a time until proper thickness is reached. Add crushed leaf buds.

To Serve

Arrange the green beans over the hirosu balls, nap with kinome an, garnish with kinome sprigs.

July Yakimono *Suzuki Uni-yaki* P. 81

Grilled Sea Bass with Sea Urchin Roe SERVES 4

10oz (280g) 1/2 fillet of sea bass
4 1/4oz (120g) fresh sea urchin roe
Flour as needed
Salt
Vegetable oil
A little *tade* paste (see grilled *ayu* recipe)

1. Cut the sea bass fillet into 4 pieces, remove any small bones with tweezers and lightly salt. Let rest for 30 minutes.

2. Make slices across the fish about 1/3" (8mm) apart and down to the skin; taking care not to cut the skin itself. Skewer the pieces parallel to the slices and the stick another couple of bamboo skewers perpendicular to those to support the fillets well. Lightly flour the skin side.

3. Ladle hot oil over the skin a couple of times. Turn and pour oil over the meat once. Transfer the fish to the grill and broil on both sides. Repeat this process twice until the skin becomes crunchy.

4. Remove the bamboo skewers and insert fresh sea urchin roe between the slices, then quickly brown under a salamander. Garnish with a little tade paste and serve with sudachi halves.

June Hiyashi-bachi *Kamo Rosu* P. 81

Roast Duck Breast SERVES 4

1 duck breast
"A" stock (1/2 cup (110ml) sake, 1/2 cup (110ml) water, 4 teaspoons regular soy sauce, 2 teaspoons light soy sauce and 1/2 Tablespoon sugar)

1. Trim duck meat and remove sinews and extra

fat. Slice the surface of the skin lengthwise every ¼" (7mm), do the same crosswise.

2. In a frying pan, sauté the breast, skin-side down, to render out excess fat. When browned immediately take the meat out and plunge into iced water. When cool, take out of water and pat dry with a towel.

3. Combine "A" stock ingredients in a pan, bring to a boil and pour into a bowl. Put the duck meat into the stock and then set the bowl in a steamer. Cover the bowl with plastic wrap and steam for 3 to 4 minutes.

4. Turn the meat over and steam three more minutes.

5. Take the meat out of the stock and cool on a wire rack. Cover with a moist towel so the meat does not dry out.

6. Cool the stock and strain. Put the meat back into the stock and refrigerate for 5 to 6 hours.

White *zuiki* (taro stems)

7oz (200g) taro stems
3qts (3L) warm water
7oz (200g) *daikon oroshi* (grated white radish)
3 *taka no tsume* (dried Japanese chili peppers)
3 tablespoons rice vinegar

"B" stock (1 pint (500ml) *dashi*, 4 teaspoon light soy sauce, 2 tablespoons *mirin* and
½ teaspoon (3g) salt)

1. Peel the thin skin of the taro stems and slice thinly lengthwise.

2. Combine warm water, grated daikon radish, dried chilies and vinegar, bring to a boil. Add taro stems and cook until tender. Plunge the cooked taro stems i0nto cold water and let cool, reserve stock

3. Drain the taro stems well and tie 3 to 4 lengths together with kitchen string.

4. Bring "B" stock to a boil and drop the taro stem bundles into the pot, remove quickly and let them cool on a rack. Chill the stock immediately, and when cooled, put the taro stems in the stock and refrigerate for 5 to 6 hours.

For *ko-imo* (small taro yams)

8 *ko-imo* (small taro yams)
Water reserved from rice rinsing
"C" stock (1⅔ cups (400ml) *dashi*, /2oz (15g) sugar, 2 tablespoons *mirin*, 1 teaspoon light soy sauce, and ½ teaspoon (3g) salt)
0.35oz (10g) dried bonito flakes

1. Cut off the top and bottom of the taro yams and scrape the skin off with a knife.

2. Bring the rice water to a boil, blanch the yams. Remove the yams and drop into a sauce pan of cold water. Change water several times. Then bring the cold water to a boil again.

3. Combine the yams and "C" stock in a sauce pan, bring to a boil, cover with a drop lid made of dried bonito flakes wrapped in gauze and cook until soft. Let cool.

Snow peas

8 snow peas
"D" stock
(6 Tablespoons (90ml) *dashi*, ½ teaspoon *usukuchi*

shoyu (light soy sauce) a little salt)

1. Stem and string the snow peas and cut them into 1¾" (4cm) long pieces.

2. Blanch snow peas in boiling salted water. Drain and quickly cool the peapods in "D" stock that has been boiled and cooled.

3. Chill the stock and when well cooled soak the pea pods in it for 5 to 6 hours in the refrigerator.

To serve

Slice the roasted duck, and arrange with taro stems, small taro yams and snow peas on a plate with a small amount of whole grain Dijon mustard.

June *Gohan* *Tsukemono-zushi*　　　　P. 82

Pickle Sushi　　　　SERVES 4

1 *senryo nasu* (Japanese egg-plant)
2lbs (1k) *nukamiso* rice bran pickling medium
2 *myoga* (ginger blossoms)
Sea salt
6oz (160g) Sushi rice (see basic recipes)
Tosa-zu (see basic recipes)
Sushi-*zu* rice vinegar (see basic recipes)
2 *shiso* leaves
A large pinch of toasted sesame seeds
A little prepared Japanese mustard (or Colemans mustard)

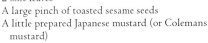

1. Cut the top and bottom off the eggplant and then make a vertical cut almost all the way through. Spread rice bran pickling medium inside, fold and cover with the rest of the pickling medium. Put a weight on top and let pickle for one or more days.

2. Cut the myoga in a half lengthways and cook in boiling water with a little vinegar. Remove and salt lightly; when cooled, soak in Tosa-zu.

3. Remove the core of the myoga. Divide ⅔oz (20g) of sushi rice into 4 pieces, top with myoga and mold into an oblong shape.

4. Cut a diamond pattern into the eggplant skin. Mix 2⅘oz (80g) sushi rice with finely chopped shiso leaves and toasted sesame seeds. Shape the rice into a stick and put the eggplant on top. Cut the sushi into 4 pieces and apply some prepared mustard on top.

Hajikami Pickled Ginger Shoots

10 *hajikami* ginger shoots
Salt
For *hajikami* vinegar
3 tablespoons rice vinegar
¾ cup (180ml) water
2½ teaspoons (10g) sugar

1. Peel the hajikami and cut into 5" (12cm) lengths and boil in water with a little vinegar. Drain on a rack and salt lightly.

2. Combine the hajikami vinegar ingredients in a sauce pan, heat until the sugar dissolves, let cool. When cool, soak the hajikami from step 1 in the vinegar solution until pickled.

■ Summer *Mizumono*

Mitsu-mame　　　　P. 84

Mixed Sweets in Syrup　　　　SERVES 4

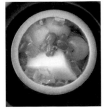

⅙ melon
1 mango
4 cherries

Simple syrup

1¼ cup (300ml) water
½ cup (100g) sugar

Bring water and sugar to a boil and leave to cool. Then chill well.

Shiratama dango (rice-flour dumplings)

1oz (30g) Sweet rice flour
2 tablespoons water

1. Add the water to the rice flour and mix well. Then divide the dough into 20 pieces and roll into balls. Boil water and drop in the dumplings. When they float to the surface, scoop them out and put in cold water. Refrigerate

Kanten (agar seaweed jelly)

¼ *kanten* stick
10 tablespoons (150ml) water
¼ cup (50g) sugar

1. Soften kanten in water

2. Combine the water, sugar and the kanten and simmer until it is reduced by ⅓.

3. Strain the liquid from step 2 and pour into a 8.5" (21cm) square pan, refrigerate to harden.

Azuki beans (sweet red beans)

1¾oz (50g) *azuki* beans
Some bamboo skin
½ cup (100g) sugar
1⅕oz (35g) *mizu ame* (millet jelly)

1. Cover beans in water and soak overnight.

2. Combine a little bamboo skin with beans and water from step 1 over low heat. Simmer beans until soft.

3. When beans are softened, divide sugar into 3 portions. Stir in the first portion, when incorporated, add the second portion and so on. Finally, stir in the mizu ame syrup and cook a little more, let cool.

Final preparation

1. Cut the *kanten* jelly into ⅜" (1cm) cubes.
2. Remove the seeds and skin from the melon and mango, and cut into bite-size pieces.

To serve

Put the melon, mango, *kanten* and red beans into a bamboo cylinder and pour in simple syrup. Top with rice-flour dumplings and cherries.

Uji-kintoki　　　　P. 84

Shaved Ice with Green Tea Syrup

Green Tea Syrup

0.35oz (10g) Green Tea Powder
9oz (2.50g) sugar

2/3 cup (150ml) water
2oz (60g) rice flour for dumpling
4 tablespoons minus 1 teaspoon water
Shaved ice
Sweet *azuki* bean paste (see mitsu-mame recipe)

To make sugar syrup

1. Boil sugar and water until the sugar is dissolved, and leave to cool. Chill well.

2. Mix the green tea powder with the syrup from step 1 and strain to remove lumps.

Rice flour dumplings

1. Add water little by little to the rice flour to make a soft dough. Divide into 12 pieces and roll into balls. Drop in boiling water and when they rise to the top, quickly remove to a bowl of cold water to cool.

To serve

Arrange a mound of shaved ice, rice-flour dumplings and a scoop of sweet red bean paste in small bowl. Drench with green tea syrup.

FALL

■ September *Hassun*

Tai Kikka-zushi   P. 89

Sea Bream Chrysanthemum Sushi   SERVES 4

3oz (80g) sushi rice (see basic recipes)
2oz (60g) *Tai*, sea bream fillets 15g per serving
Yuzu as needed
Chrysanthemum blossoms pickled with *Tosa-zu* (see basic recipes)
Pickling vinegar as needed (see basic recipes)

1. Combine prepared sushi rice with the chrysanthemum blossoms pickled in Tosa-zu and season with a squeeze of yuzu juice. Divide into 4 portions and shape into balls.

2. Soak the sea bream fillets in the vinegar for about 20 minutes.

3. Dry the sea bream from step 2 on a kitchen towel, remove the skin and slice into thin square pieces

4. Place a slice of fish on a moist towel, top with a ball of sushi rice, wrap and shape into a ball. Garnish each sushi with pickled chrysanthemum blossoms at the center.

Hamo Hachiman-maki

Hamo and Gobo Roll   YIELDS 2 STICKS

1 hamo cut into 2 fillets
1oz (30g) *gobo* root (a thin one)
"A" stock (1/3 cup (70ml) sake and 4 teaspoons light soy sauce)
"B" stock (2 cups sake (500ml,) 1qt (1l) *dashi*, 10

Tablespoons regular soy sauce, 2 1/2 Tablespoons sugar and 1/3 cup (75ml) *mirin*)

1. Prepare the hamo fillets as per p.68.

2. Cut the gobo into pieces 1/5" (5mm) square and 4" (10cm) long. Cook in "A" stock.

3. Wrap 3 or 4 gobo sticks from step 2 with the hamo fillets (skin side toward the stick) and when the fillet is rolled around the sticks two or three times, tie with kitchen string. Make another stick in the same way.

4. Bring "B" stock in a pan to a boil and simmer the hamo rolls from step 3 for 10–15 minutes and let cool. Cut into serving pieces.

Ebi Matsukaze

Shrimp Cake

YIELDS A 8.5"/21cm SQUARE CONTAINER

1 3/4 lbs (800g) *kuruma ebi*, medium shrimp
14oz (400g) fish paste or ground shrimp
1 teaspoon *kuzu* dissolved in water
1 egg
3 egg yolks
1 teaspoon regular soy sauce
1 teaspoon light soy sauce
Poppy seeds for decoration

1. Cut half of the shrimp into 3/8" (1cm) pieces. Sprinkle with regular soy sauce.

2. Puree the rest of the shrimp, fish paste, dissolved kuzu, egg yolks, egg and light soy sauce in a food processor.

3. In a bowl, combine the chopped shrimp from step 1 and the paste from step 2. Transfer to an 8"/21cm square container lined with cooking paper. Sprinkle with poppy seeds. Bake in a 300°F (150°C) oven for 40 minutes. Let cool and cut into serving pieces.

Yakime Kuri Chakin

Wrapped Chestnut

17.5oz (500g) baked chestnuts (peeled)
3/5 cup (150ml) water
4 1/2 Tablespoons (55g) sugar

1. Bring water and sugar to a boil and let cool.

2. Puree the peeled chestnuts in a food processor while pouring the syrup from step 1 in a slow stream.

3. Take a 1/2oz (15g) serving of the chestnut paste, shape into a ball using a moist towel. Bake the chestnut balls in a 350F (180C) degree oven until brown.

Icho Imo

Ginkgo Sweet Potato

See recipe for October

Garasa Ebi Laochu-zuke no Sudachi-gama/ Masu no Ko

Grass Shrimps in Shaoxing Rice Wine with Trout Roe   YIELDS 1.6lbs (750g)

3 1/3lbs (1.5k) grass shrimp
1 1/10 cup (275ml) Shaoxing rice wine (with alcohol evaporated)

1/2oz (15g) *kombu*
1 cup (250ml) Tosa soy sauce (see basic recipes)
1 2/3 (50g) scallions
1 2/3 (50g) ginger grated
4 dried Japanese chili peppers
Trout roe for decoration
Nikiri-zake

1. Peel and de-vein shrimp while they are still alive. Rinse with water and towel dry. Sprinkle with salt and refrigerate for a day.

2. Macerate kombu in the Shaoxing rice wine for a day.

3. Combine the Tosa soy sauce, scallions, ginger, dried Japanese chili peppers, Shaoxing rice wine and Shrimp from step 1 and marinate.

4. Soak trout roe in nikiri-zake for 20–30 seconds to remove salt.

5. Cut off the top of sudachi, make a chrysanthemum shaped cut and scoop out the insides.

6. Fill the sudachi cups with drained shrimps from step 3 and top with the trout roe from step 4.

Shio Kofuki Ginnan

Salted Ginkgo Nuts   SERVES 4

32 ginkgo nuts
1 1/4 cups (300ml) water
1 teaspoon (5g) salt

1. Crack and peel ginkgo nuts.

2. Put the ginkgo nuts from step 1 in a pot with water and salt. Cook until the liquid is completely reduced, shaking the pan so as not to burn the nuts.

Matsuba Somen

Green Tea Noodle Fans

See October recipes

October *Sakizuke*   *Kabura Furofuki*   P. 90

Turnips with Miso Sauce   SERVES 10

10 1 2/3oz kabura turnips peeled
1 sheet *kombu* 2"/5cm square
Stock (2 1/2 cups (600ml) *dashi*, 2 1/2 cups (600ml) turnip cooking liquid, 2 Tablespoons *mirin*, 4 teaspoons light soy sauce and 1/2 tablespoon salt)
Dried bonito flakes as needed

Walnut miso paste as needed
Walnut meat (peeled and baked until brown) as needed
Grated *yuzu* skin for garnish

Small turnips

1. Cut off the tops and bottoms of the small turnips and pare them into 1 3/4oz (50g) pieces.

2. Combine kombu and plenty of water in a pot and simmer the turnips with a drop lid until a bamboo skewer easily pierces them. When cooked, remove the kombu.

3. Bring stock to a boil, add cooked turnips and let them steep for 7–8 minutes.

4. Place the turnips on a plate and sauce with walnut miso paste (about 1 tablespoon per person). Top with crushed walnuts and grated yuzu skin.

Walnut *miso* paste

9oz (250g) ground walnuts (see basic recipes)
2.5oz (75g) ground sesame seeds (see basic recipes)
17.5oz (500g) *taki-mi*so cooked miso paste (see basic recipes.)
1¼ cup (300ml) *nikiri-zake*
3oz (100ml) walnut oil

Combine ground walnuts and sesame seeds and add cooked miso paste and mix well. Thin by gradually stirring in nikiri-zake and walnut oil.

September *Sakizuke* **Kurumi-dofu**   P. 90

Walnut Tofu
YIELDS A 8.5"/21cm SQUARE CONTAINER

7½ cups (1.8l) *dashi*
6oz (170g) *kuzu* (*Kumakawa hon-kuzu*)
3⅓oz (100g) ground walnuts (see basic recipes)
3⅓oz (100g) ground sesame seeds (see basic recipes)
1 tablespoon walnut oil
4oz (120g) chopped walnuts
2 teaspoon light soy sauce
A little salt

For *kuidashi* jelly

Stock (1¾ cups (420ml) *dashi*, 4 Tablespoons light soy sauce and 4 Tablespoons *mirin*)
Dried bonito flakes as needed
½ Tablespoon (7.5g) gelatin powder
Grated *wasabi* to taste
Delaware grapes
Hanaho jiso shiso buds

1. Combine ground sesame seeds, ground walnuts and kuzu with dashi and push the mixture through a fine drum screen.

2. Heat the mixture from step 1 in a saucepan, add a little salt, stir continuously with a wooden paddle.

3. When it starts to thicken, lower heat and keep stirring the mixture vigorously for about 20 minutes. Add light soy sauce and walnut oil to the walnut paste and mix well.

4. Pour it into an 8.5"/21cm square container, cover with a glass plate and chill in a pan of ice water. When cool, refrigerate overnight.

5. Cut the kurumi dofu into serving pieces and spoon the kuidashi jelly combined with grated wasabi over it. Top with 3 peeled grapes, 2 unpeeled grapes and shiso buds.

For *kuidashi* jelly

1. Combine the stock in a pan and bring to a boil, then turn off the fire and add the dried bonito flakes (*oi-gatsuo*). Let cool and strain.

2. Combine the stock from step 1 and the gelatin powder in a saucepan and heat. When the gelatin is dissolved, turn off the heat and let cool. Refrigerate overnight and strain through a screen.

September *Nimono-wan* **Honen-wan**   P. 93

Harvest Soup
SERVES 4

4 1oz (25g) pieces prepared *hamo* filets (see note on *hamo* preparation on page 68)
Toasted rice as needed
Egg white as needed
Vegetable oil for frying
¼ bunch *mibuna* greens
1 small *matsutake* mushroom

"A" stock for *mibuna* (6 Tablespoons (90ml) *dashi*, ½ teaspoon light soy sauce and a little salt)

For *tomago-dofu* egg tofu

8 eggs
1¾ cups (400ml) *dashi*
2 tablespoons light soy sauce

"B" stock for *hamo* (27fl oz (800ml) *dashi*, 2 tablespoons light soy sauce and salt to taste)
"C" stock for *matsutake* and soup (2½ cups (600ml) *dashi*, 1 tablespoon light soy sauce ½ teaspoon salt)

Yellow *yuzu* as needed

1. Prepare egg tofu: beat the eggs and add the dashi to the eggs, mix well and strain. Season with light soy sauce and pour into an 8.5"/21cm square container, steam for 20 minutes. When cooled, punch out crescent moon-shapes.

2. Blanch mibuna and plunge into ice water to cool. Soak in "A" stock for a half day. Form a bundle of mibuna ½" (1to 1.5cm) in diameter and cut into 1⅓" (3.5cm) pieces.

3. Rinse the hamo, fillet it and slice through tiny bones. Cut it into 1oz (25g) pieces. Dip the meat side in egg whites and dredge in toasted rice. Deep-fry hamo pieces and drain.

4. Simmer the hamo from step 3 in "B" stock for about 10 minutes.

5. Clean matsutake and cut into serving-size pieces. Simmer in "C" stock.

6. Combine the 2 stocks from steps 4 and 5 and adjust the seasoning to for soup.

7. Place the hamo, egg tofu, mibuna, and matsutake in a bowl and cover with hot soup from step 6. Garnish with a thin julienne of yuzu skin.

November *Sakizuke* **Kumoko Gin-an-mushi**   P. 93

Steamed Cod Roe with Silver Sauce
SERVES 10

14oz (400g) *kumoko*, cod roe
3 chives
Ginger juice as needed

Gin-an silver sauce (1¾ cups (400ml) *dashi*, 1 tablespoon light soy sauce, 1 teaspoon *mirin* and a little salt)
Kuzu or corn starch dissolved in water as needed

1. Quickly rinse the cod roe in highly salted water and cut into bite-size pieces. Boil them in fresh water, then soak in 2% salt water for an hour, drain.

2. Bring the silver sauce ingredients to a boil in a saucepan and stir in the kuzu mixture to make a thick sauce.

3. Place the cod roe from step 1 and the silver sauce from step 2 in a small bowl and steam until the cod roe is heated through. To serve, sprinkle with ginger juice and garnish with finely chopped chives.

■ October *Hassun*

Kamazu Yakime-zushi   P. 94

Barracuda Sushi
SERVES 8

7oz (200g) *kamasu* (a type of small barracuda) fillet
5⅓oz (150g) sushi rice (see basic recipes)
Salt
Vinegar for pickling (see basic recipes)
1 *sudachi*

1. Rinse kamasu fillet, remove any small bones with fish tweezers and sprinkle with salt. Let fillets rest for 2 to 3 hours.

2. Make a stick-shaped sushi with the rice.

3. Soak the kamasu from step 1 in the vinegar for about 5 minutes and dry with a kitchen towel, Slice the surface of the skin and sear the skin with a propane torch. Cover with a damp towel to cool immediately.

4. Slice the thick part of the kamasu from step 3 and put it on a wet towel skin-side down. Cover with sushi stick from step 2 and lightly compress.

5. Cut the sushi from the step 4 into 8 pieces and between pieces, garnish with thinly sliced *sudachi*.

Ayu Shirako to Mako Uruka no Sudachi-gama/ Masu no Ko

Salted Ayu Entrails with Trout Roe
SERVES 4

2oz (60g) *ayu uruka*, *shirako* (milt)
⅔oz (20g) *ayu uruka*, *mako* (ovaries)
Ao yuzu, green yuzu citrus skin as needed
Sudachi juice to taste
Light soy sauce to taste

Masu no ko, trout roe as needed
Nikiri-zake as needed

4 *sudachi*

1. Depending on how salty they are, soak the ayu entrails in several changes of water and sake (water 1:1 sake). Clean and de-vein the shirako and mako and chop.

2. Soak the trout roe in nikiri-zake for about 20 to 30 seconds to remove salt.

3. Combine the mako and shirako from step 1, and season with sudachi juice, grated yuzu skin and light soy sauce.

4. Hollow out the sudachi. Place the ingredients from step 4 into a sudachi cup and top with the trout roe from step 3.

Yakime Guri
Grilled chestnuts
SERVES 4

4 chestnuts
Kuchinashi, gardenia flowers as needed
2oz (70g) sugar
3/4 cup (180ml) water

1. Peel the chestnuts completely.
2. Crush the gardenias and wrap in gauze, then drop into boiling water. When the water turns yellow, drop in the chestnuts and let them soak for 10 minutes. Drain well and brown them under a toaster oven or broiler.
3. Bring the water and sugar to a boil and cook the chestnuts in the syrup 30 minutes.

Hamo no Ko Rakugan
Hamo Roe Mousse
YIELDS A 6"/15CM SQUARE CONTAINER

15oz (420g) *hamo* roe
Stock (1 cup (240ml) sake, 1 cup (240ml) water, 2 teaspoons light soy sauce, 2 teaspoons *mirin*)
4 1/2oz (125g) ground *hamo* meat
1/2 egg
1/2 egg yolk
3oz (100g) *yurine*, lily bulb (cleaned, steamed and salted)
1/2 teaspoon light soy sauce

1. Rinse hamo roe in a strainer, remove membrane and drain well.
2. Cook the roe from step 1 with the stock until the liquid is totally reduced, then cool
3. Mix hamo roe from step 2, ground fish, egg, egg yolk and soy sauce in the food processor.
4. Add lily bulb pieces to paste from step 3 and pour into a container, steam. When cooled, cut into serving pieces.

Icho Imo
Ginkgo Sweet Potato
SERVES 4

Sweet potato; as much as needed
Yellow food coloring; a few drops

1. Cut the sweet potatoes into about 1/12" (2mm) thick slices, and punch with a ginkgo-shape mold. Soak them in water with yellow food coloring for a day
2. Towel dry the potatoes from step 1 and let dry for about a half day.
3. Deep-fry them on low heat and salt lightly.

Hisui Ginnan
Jade Ginkgo Nuts
SERVES 4

12 *ginnan*, ginkgo nuts
7 tablespoons (100ml) water
7 tablespoons (100ml) sake
1/2 teaspoon (3g) salt

1. Crack and peel the ginkgo nuts.
2. Combine all ingredients in a saucepan and simmer until the liquid reduced, shaking the pan at the end so the nuts don't burn.

Matsuba Somen
Green Tea Noodle Fans
SERVES 4

2 small bunches of *cha-somen*, green tea somen noodles
Yaki-nori, toasted seaweed, as needed
Egg white, as needed

1. Cut the noodles into 2" (5cm) lengths.
2. Cut the *nori* into 3/8" (1cm) square pieces.
3. Make two small bundles of somen noodles and wrap a nori band dipped in egg white around the middle. Deep-fry on low heat 320F (160C), remove and drain. Cut in half at the nori band to make 4 pieces.

■ November *Hassun*
Wari-zansho Yuzu-gama Mori   P. 96
Yuzu Sansho Cup
SERVES 10

Monkfish liver

17oz (500g) *Ankimo* monk-fish liver
1 *taka no tsume*, dried Japanese chili pepper
4" ('10cm) white leek
1/3oz (10g) *yuzu* skin
1/3oz (10g) ginger
Stock (3 cups (720ml) sake, 1 1/2 cups (360ml) water, 4/5 cups (200ml) *mirin*, 3/5 cup (160ml) regular soy sauce and 5 Tablespoons light soy sauce)

1. Peel the membrane of the monkfish liver, lightly salt and refrigerate for 12 hours.
2. Slice the ginger and grill the white leek. Remove the pith from the *yuzu* skin. Remove the seeds from *taka no tsume*.
3. Roll the monkfish liver from step 1 in cheese cloth. Tie both of the edges with rubber bands and shape like salami.
4. Put the ingredients from step 2 and 3 in a bowl.
5. Heat the stock in a sauce pan. When it boils and the alcohol has evaporated, pour the stock into the bowl from step 4 and wrap in plastic film. Cook for 20 minutes in a steamer on high heat. Let cool and slice in serving pieces.

Mibuna

1/2 bunch *mibuna* Japanese greens
Stock (1 1/2 cups (360ml) *dashi*, 2 teaspoons light soy sauce and 1/3 teaspoon salt)

1. Cut off the mibuna roots and tie into bundles with rubber bands. Rinse the mibuna and quickly blanch in boiling water. Plunge into ice water and drain well.
2. Put the stock in a pan on the fire and when it boils, turn of heat and let cool.
3. Soak the mibuna from step 2 in the cool stock.

Shimeji mushrooms

1 2/3oz (50g) *shimeji* mushrooms
Stock (5 Tablespoons (90ml) *dashi*, 1 teaspoon light soy sauce and 1/2 teaspoon *mirin*)

1. Divide shimeji mushroom into small portions.
2. Put the stock and shimeji mushroom from step 1 in a pan and cook XX. Let cool.

5 ki yuzu, yellow yuzu

1. Cut yuzu into halves and hollow out. Cut into a sansho-shape.
2. Place monkfish liver, mibuna and shimeji mushrooms in the yuzu cup from step 1.

Momiji Ika
Autumn Leaves Squid

10 1/2oz (300g) *ika*, squid
1 3/4oz (50g) *shio uni*, salted sea urchin roe
1 egg yolk
2/3oz 20ml *nikiri-zake*
a little *mirin*

1. Strain the salted sea urchin roe. Combine the egg yolk, nikiri-zake and mirin with the sea urchin roe and mix well.
2. Rinse the squid well, peel its outer membrane, skewer and broil. When nearly cooked, brush the sauce from step 1 on the squid and broil on low heat taking care not to burn. Repeat this process a couple of times.
3. When ready cut into shapes with a maple leaf shaped die.

Karasumi
Cured Mullet Roe

2.8oz (80g) *karasumi*, dried mullet roe
Peel the membrane and slice into 1/5" inch (5mm) thick slices.

Kombu Kago
Kombu Basket

10 *kombu kago*, kombu baskets (available at grocery stores in Japan)
Deep-fry the kombu basket on low heat.

Kamo Kimo Matsukaze
Duck Liver Terrine

2lb (1kg duck) liver paste
1/2lb (250g) *sakura miso* red miso paste
7oz (200g) ground fish meat
7oz (200g) *yamaimo* mountain yam (grated)
13 1/2fl oz (400ml) fresh cream
2/3 box unsalted butter
About 7 Tablespoons Cognac
1/2lb (225g) raisins (marinated in Cognac overnight)
2oz (60g) (pine nuts rinsed and toweled dried, baked in a 230°F (110°C) oven for 15 minutes.)
Poppy seeds for garnish

Duck liver paste

6.6lbs 3kg fresh duck liver
Stock (2 1/2 cups (600ml) sake, 2 1/2 cups (600ml) water, 6 Tablespoons, regular soy sauce and 2 1/2 Tablespoons)

1. Rinse duck liver a couple times and transfer to a sieve. Leave to drain overnight to remove blood.
2. Put the liver from step 1 in a shallow container or

bowl and cover with boiled stock. Seal with plastic film and steam in a steamer for one hour.

3. Strain the liver from step 2 to make a paste.

4. Combine sakura miso paste, eggs, ground meat, the paste from step 3, grated yams, fresh cream, melted butter, Cognac in a food processor.

5. Transfer the mixture from step 4 to a bowl and add pine nuts and raisins and mix well. Pour it into a terrine, sprinkle with poppy seeds and bake in a 300°F (150°C) oven for an hour.

Kuwai Senbei
Water Chestnut Crackers   SERVES 5
(not pictured)

5 *kuwai*, a vegetable similar to a water chestnut
Vegetable oil for frying
A pinch of salt

1. Peel and pare the kuwai into a six-sided shape and slice them. Soak in water for a while, drain well. Let dry overnight on a screen.

2. Deep-fry slices at 320F–340F (160°C–170°C) and sprinkle lightly with salt.

Kuri Senbei
Chestnut Crackers   SERVES 8
(not pictured)

8 *kuri*, chestnuts, peeled
Vegetable oil for frying
A pinch of salt

1. Slice the chestnuts and soak in water for a while, drain well. Spread on a screen to dry overnight.

2. Deep-fry them at 320°F–340°F (160°C–170°C) and sprinkle lightly with salt.

Shio Kofuki Ginnan
Salted Ginkgo Nuts

See September recipes

Matsuba Somen
Green Tea Noodle Fans

See September recipes

■ Fall *Mukozuke*

Tsubasu   P. 98
Young Yellowtail

Tsubasu young yellowtail,
Sudachi
salt

Fillet the *tsubasu*, remove the outer skin and slice. To serve, garnish with sudachi and salt.

Saba   P. 100
Mackerel

1 ¹/₂lbs (700g) *aki saba* autumn mackerel

shime-zu pickling vinegar as needed (see basic recipes)

Garnish

Udo (Japanese spikenard) and carrots cut in thin spirals
Pon-zu (see basic recipes)
Grated ginger

1. Rinse and fillet the mackerel.

2. Remove small bones with tweezers and sprinkle well with salt, then let rest for about 30 minutes.

3. Towel dry and marinate fillets in the pickling vinegar for about 15 minutes.

4. Dry, peel the outer skin, make cuts on the inner skin and slice into serving pieces.

5. Garnish with udo and carrot spirals. Serve with pon-zu and grated ginger.

October *Futamono*   *Matsutake Dobin-mushi*   P. 102
Steamed Matsutake Teapot   SERVES 4

3 ¹/₃oz (100g) *hamo*
4oz (120g) *matsutake* mushrooms
Mitsuba to taste
Stock (³/₅ cup (140ml) *dashi*, ²/₅ cup (100ml) *mirin*, and 3 Tablespoons light soy sauce)
A little grated yuzu skin
A little regular soy sauce
2 *sudachi*

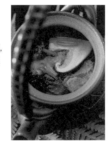

1. Slice hamo through tiny bones (see note on *hamo* preparation on page 68) and cut into 4 pieces, then cut the pieces in half.

2. Remove the hard part of *matsutake* mushroom stems and wipe with a wet towel.

3. Remove the leaves from mitsuba and cut the stems into ³/₄" (1.5cm) lengths.

4. Bring the stock in a pan to a boil and adjust the taste.

5. Arrange the hamo and *matsutake* mushrooms in an individual serving pot and pour the soup from step 4 and put on the heat. When the matsutake stems have softened, add the mitsuba, sprinkle with grated yuzu skin and add a few drops of regular soy sauce to taste. Serve with a half sudachi.

November *Futamono*   *Wakasa Guji Awa-mushi*   P. 104
Tilefish Steamed with Millet   SERVES 10

10 1oz (35g) pieces *guji* tilefish fillets
3oz (100g) *awa* millet
1oz (35 g) *domyoji* glutinous rice steamed, dried and toasted roughly
4 *shiitake* mushrooms
12 chestnuts
¹/₂ bunch *kikuna* edible chrysanthemum greens
10 *aomi daikon* thin Kyoto radish
¹/₃ *kintoki ninjin* red Kyoto carrot
1 *ki yuzu* yellow *yuzu*

"A" stock for shiitake mushrooms (³/₄ cup (180ml) dashi, 2 teaspoons light soy sauce)
"B" stock for flavoring aomi daikon, carrots, and chrysanthemum leaves (3 cups (720ml) dashi, 4 teaspoons light soy sauce and ¹/₄ Tablespoon salt)
"C" stock for millet and domyoji (10 Tablespoons (150ml) dashi, 1 teaspoon light soy sauce and a little salt)
"D" stock for soup (1qt (1L) dashi, 5 teaspoons light soy sauce, 1 teaspoon salt, 1 Tablespoon *mirin*)
Kuzu starch dissolved in water as needed

1. Remove the hard bottom of shiitake mushroom stems, cut mushrooms into sixths and simmer in the "A" stock.

2. Peel the chestnuts, cut into ¹/₃" dice (7mm) and cook in boiling salted water.

3. Pare the aomi daikon into baby carrot shapes. Boil them until tender, then plunge into ice water.

4. Cut the carrot into ¹/₈" (3mm) square sticks about 4" (10cm) long. Sprinkle with a little salt and when softened, tie two of them together using another carrot stick as a string, soak in water to remove the salt, then blanch them in boiling water, plunge into ice water.

5. Drain the daikon from step 3 and carrots from step 4 and soak in the "B" stock.

6. Remove the leaves from the chrysanthemum stalks. Blanch stalks to brighten their color, plunge into ice water, drain and finely chop. Soak them in the "B" stock.

7. Rinse the tilefish and fillet. Remove the skin and small bones. Sprinkle with salt and let rest for 30 minutes. Slice into 10 1oz (35g) each) pieces. Butterfly the slices to wrap around *awa* millet dumplings.

8. Combine the awa millet and domyoji in a bowl with the boiled "C" stock and mix well. Seal the bowl with plastic wrap and steam for about 10 minutes.

9. Divide the mixture into 10 (1oz (30g) each) portions. Wrap pieces of shiitake and chestnut with the mixture and cover and wrap them with the slice of tilefish.

10. Bring the D stock ingredients to a boil and thicken with the kuzu mixture, then add the drained chopped chrysanthemum stalks from step 6 to make a sauce

11. Put the rolls from step 9 in a bowl and cook in a steamer. Place warmed aomi daikon and tied carrot in a bowl. Cover with the sauce from step 10 and garnish with a fine julienne of yuzu skin.

October *Yakimono*   *Kamasu Sugiita-yaki*   P. 106
Planked Barracuda   SERVES 10

5 12oz (350g) *kamasu*, barracuda
10 *shiitake* mushrooms
20 *sugiita* (very thin strips of cedar wood)
Bamboo skin strips for tying
5 *sudachi*
Miso yuanji (see basic recipes)

1. Rinse the barracudas and fillet, removing small bones with tweezers. Lightly salt and let rest for a couple of hours.

2. Dry the barracuda fillets from step 1 with a towel and cure them in the miso paste for 12 hours.

3. Remove the stems from the shiitake mushrooms and salt lightly.

4. Place a folded barracuda fillet on a piece of cedar that has been soaked in water. Put a shiitake mushroom on the top and cover with another cedar piece. Bind with a piece of bamboo skin string.

5. Bake at 340°F (170°C) for about 15 to 20 minutes. Singe and light the cedar pieces on fire with a propane torch. Garnish with a half sudachi. To eat, season with a squeeze of sudachi juice.

September *Yakimono* *Komochi Ayu* P. 108

Ayu with Roe

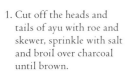

Ayu with roe
Salt
Tade-zu (see the recipe on page 172)

1. Cut off the heads and tails of ayu with roe and skewer, sprinkle with salt and broil over charcoal until brown.

2. When it is broiled, remove the skewers and backbone.

3. Serve immediately with tade-zu.

Walnuts simmered in syrup

10-¹⁄₂oz 300g walnuts (shelled)
Syrup (1qt (1l) sake, 7 Tablespoons (100ml) regular soy sauce, 2–3 Tablespoons light soy sauce, 6 Tablespoons (70g) sugar, 10-¹⁄₂oz (300g) *mizu ame* millet syrup)
Vegetable oil for frying

1. Deep-fry walnuts.

2. Make the syrup: heat the syrup ingredients in a pan and evaporate the alcohol and simmer until the liquid is reduced to a syrup (take care not to simmer so long that it becomes hard).

3. Coat the walnuts from step 1 with 150g of the syrup.

November *Yakimono* *Kamo Hoba-yaki* P. 110

Duck Grilled on a Magnolia Leaf SERVES 4

1 duck breast
4 chestnuts
Stock (³⁄₄ cup (180ml) *dashi*, 1 teaspoon light soy sauce, 1 teaspoon *mirin*, Dash (1g) of 1g salt)
12 jade ginkgo nuts (see recipe on p. 176)
300g hoba miso paste (recipe below)
White part of *aonegi* Japanese leeks as needed
Scallions as needed
Yuzu as needed
4 magnolia leaves

1. Remove sinews and extra fat from the duck breast. Slice the surface of the skin lengthwise every ¼" (7mm) Do the same crosswise. Sauté the breast

skin side down to render out excess fat. Let cool and slice.

2. Peel chestnuts and simmer in the stock.

3. Cook the ginkgo nuts as per jade ginkgo nuts recipe (p. 176).

4. Cut aonegi and scallions into very fine slices and soak in water. Drain and combine with julienned yuzu skin.

5. Soak magnolia leaves in water before putting on heat.

6. Place a portion of hoba miso on each magnolia leaf from step 5 and place on top of an individual Japanese charcoal stove at the table. Put the ginkgo nuts, chestnut, duck breast on the miso and top with the combined green onions, leeks and yuzu skin from step 4. Eat as soon as the duck meat is cooked.

Hoba Miso Paste

3¹⁄₃oz (100g) *sakura* miso paste
12¹⁄₂oz (350g) Saikyo miso white miso
1¹⁄₅ cups (270ml) sake
1 egg yolk
A little sesame seed paste
¹⁄₂ Tablespoon toasted sesame seed oil

Combine all ingredients except toasted sesame oil, mix well. Heat in a sauce pan stirring constantly so as not to burn for about 15 minutes. Finish with sesame oil and mix well.

November *Suzakana* *Kaki Namasu* P. 112

Japanese Persimmon Namasu SERVES 5

5 whole persimmons+3¹⁄₃oz (100g) peeled persimmon
14oz (400g) *daikon* giant radish
2oz (60g) carrots
¹⁄₂ bunch *mitsuba* trefoil
Julienned *yuzu* skin as needed

²⁄₃oz (20g) toasted and ground sesame seeds
¹⁄₂ cup (130ml) *Tosa-zu* flavored vinegar (see basic recipes)
¹⁄₂ teaspoon light soy sauce
¹⁄₂ teaspoon *mirin*
¹⁄₂ teaspoon *sudachi* juice

1. Cut the daikon and carrots into rectangular slices. Soak the daikon in 2% salt water and the carrots in 3% salt water.

2. Remove the leaves from the mitsuba (the leaves won't be used), blanch the stems in boiling salted water, then cut into ²⁄₃" (1.5cm) lengths.

3. Cut the 100g persimmon into rectangular slices like the daikon and carrots from step one.

4. Mix the sesame seeds, Tosa-zu, light soy sauce, mirin and sudachi juice.

5. Drain the daikon and carrots well and combine with the persimmon, and mitsuba with the sauce from step 4.

6. Hollow out 5 persimmons to make cups and place the ingredients from step 5, top with julienned yuzu skin.

September *Takiawase*
Yakinasu to Nishin Takiawase P. 114

Grilled Japanese Eggplant and Simmered Herring SERVES 4

3 *migaki nishin* fillets Dried salted herring
1 small piece ginger
"A" stock for herring (¹⁄₃ pint (160ml) sake, ¹⁄₃ pint (160ml) *dashi*, 7 Tablespoons (100ml) mirin, 1 rounded teaspoon sugar, A little more than 2 Tablespoons regular soy sauce)

2 Japanese eggplants
"B" stock for eggplant (1 ¹⁄₄ cups (300ml) *dashi*, 4 ¹⁄₂ teaspoons light soy sauce and 1 Tablespoon *mirin*)
¹⁄₅oz (5g) dried bonito flakes
¹⁄₂ bunch of *shungiku* edible chrysanthemum leaves
"C" stock for shungiku (³⁄₄ cup (180ml) *dashi*,1 teaspoon light soy sauce and a pinch (1g) salt)
1 small slice of ginger

1. Soak the migaki nishin in rice rinsing water for about 2 days, cook for 1 day in the ricewater.

2. Drain and let soak in cool water, then place in a pot, cover with fresh water, bring to a boil. Remove the bones from the nishin and steam for 10 minutes.

3. Simmer the nishin in the "A" stock with ginger for 1 day, when finished cut into serving pieces.

4. Grill the eggplant and peel. Cook slowly in the "B" stock covered with a drop lid made from dried bonito flakes wrapped in cheese cloth until the eggplants soak up the flavor.

5. Remove the shungiku leaves from stems (discard stems) and blanch them in boiling water, plunge into ice water. Drain and soak them in the "C" stock.

6. Cut the eggplants into serving pieces. Coarsely chop the shungiku.

7. Arrange items in serving bowl. Drizzle ginger juice (juice squeezed from grated ginger) and pour in some "B" stock. Garnish with finely julienned ginger.

November *Shiizakana*
Kin-tsuba Ise Ebi Shiro-miso-jitate P. 116

Golden Spiny Lobster with White Miso SERVES 10

4 *Ise ebi*, spiny lobsters
8 egg yolks
1 Shogoin turnip
1 bunch *hatakena* Kyoto mustard greens
¹⁄₆oz (5g) kombu
Vegetable oil for frying
Yellow yuzu skin as needed

"A" stock for *hatakena*, boiled once and cooled (2 ¹⁄₃ cups (540ml) *dashi* 1 Tablespoon light soy sauce ¹⁄₁₀oz (3g) salt)
"B" stock for cooking turnips (3 ¹⁄₂ cups (810ml) *dashi*, 3 ¹⁄₂ cups (810ml) turnip cooking liquid from step 2, 3 Tablespoons light soy sauce, ¹⁄₂ Tablespoon salt, 2 teaspoons *mirin* and 10g dried bonito flakes)

"C" stock for cooking lobster (2 1/2 cups (600ml) sake, 1qt (1L) *dashi*, 7 1/2oz (200g) Saikyo white miso paste)

1. Cut off the hatakena roots. Blanch hatakena in boiling salted water, plunge into ice water and soak in the "A" stock. Drain the hatekena. Roll and mold into a cylinder and cut into 2" (4cm) pieces.

2. Peel the turnip, cut into half-moon-shaped pieces and pare off the corners. Boil with kombu and plenty of water until a bamboo skewer can easily pierce them.

3. Combine the turnips with "B" stock on low heat, cover with a drop lid made from dried bonito flakes wrapped in gauze and cook.

4. Separate the heads and tails of the spiny lobsters and remove the meat from the shells. Cut the meat into about 1/2oz (15g) pieces and cut the head in half lengthways.

5. Combine the lobster heads, shells and "C" 2 1/2 cups (600ml) sake, cover with a drop lid and cook until the sake is reduced by half. Remove the heads and shells. Pour in 1qt (1L) dashi and dissolve 7 1/2oz (200g) white miso paste in it.

6. Coat the lobster meat from step 4 with the egg yolks and deep-fry them at around 340°F (170°C.) Pour boiling water over them to remove any excess oil and put in the "C" stock from step 5 and cook for a couple of minutes.

7. Place the turnip, the meat from step 6, and the warmed hatakena from step 1 in a bowl and pour the soup from step 5. Top with the yuzu julienne.

September *Naka-choko*
Hoshi Konoko Muscat Koji-zuke   P. 119

Dried Konoko with Koji-Pickled Muscat Grapes   SERVES 4

1 *bachi-ko*, dried sea cucumber ovaries
12 muscat grapes
7oz (200g) *kome koji* rice lees (see the glossary)
1 1/4 cup (300ml) sake
1 1/4 cups (300ml) *mirin*
1 teaspoon salt
A light soy sauce
A little dissolved Japanese mustard

1. Combine sake, mirin, salt and light soy sauce in a sauce pan and bring to a boil.

2. Put koji in a bowl, add the liquid from step 1 and cook for about 15 minutes in a steamer. Let cool. Add some Japanese mustard to the koji and mix well.

3. Peel the muscat grapes and remove the seeds. Pickle them in the koji from step 2 for a half day.

4. Sear bachiko right before serving.

October *Gohan*
Hamo Matsu Don   P. 120

Hamo and Matsutake Mushroom Rice Bowl   SERVES 4

1.1lb (500g) *hamo* fillets
5oz (150g) matsutake mushrooms

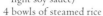

8 eggs
1 bunch mitsuba (trefoil)
Sansho powder to taste
Stock (1/3 pint (140ml) *dashi*, 7 Tablespoons (100ml) *mirin*, 3 1/2 Tablespoons light soy sauce)
4 bowls of steamed rice

1. Prepare hamo fillets as per note on page 68 and cut into serving pieces.

2. Remove the hard end of the matsutake mushroom stems and wipe with a wet towel. Cut them into a large bite-size pieces.

3. Remove and discard leaves from the mitsuba and cut into 2/3"(1.5cm) length.

4. Mix the ingredients of the stock well. Lightly beat the eggs.

5. Divide the cooked rice among 4 bowls.

6. Divide the ingredient from steps 2, 3, and 4 into 4 portions since each dish is cooked individually in a small frying pan. Bring the stock, the sliced mushrooms and hamo to a boil. When cooked, sprinkle with mitsuba stems and first pour a half portion (1 egg) of beaten egg into the pan, then pour on the rest (1 egg). When eggs are barely set, arrange the mixture over a bowl of hot rice. Sprinkle with sansho powder to taste.

■ Fall *Mizumono*
Kabosu Sorbet   P. 122

Kabosu Sorbet
YIELDS 2qts (2l)

2 cups (500ml) water
2 cups (500ml) milk
2 cups (500ml) *kabosu* juice
2 1/2 cups (500g) granulated sugar
2 *kabosu* peels

1. Bring water, granulated sugar, and kabosu skin to a boil in a pan. Turn off the heat and leave to cool. When cooled remove the skin.

2. Mix the syrup from step 1, kabosu juice and milk and freeze in an ice-cream maker.

Ichijiku-kan   P. 122

Fig Jelly
YIELDS AN 8.5"/21cm SQUARE CONTAINER

1 3/4 lbs (800g) fig paste (see below)
3 2/5 cups (800ml) water
3 1/3 Tablespoons sugar
1 1/3oz (40g) pearl agar (made of agar seaweed and used for hardening)
A little cinnamon powder

1. Heat all of the ingredients except cinnamon powder in a pan and mix well.

2. When sugar and pearl agar are dissolved, add cinnamon powder and mix well. Pour it into a 8.5"/21cm square container, cover with plate of glass and chill in ice water.

3. When it hardens, remove from the container and cut into serving pieces.

Fig paste
50 figs
3 cups (720ml) water
1 4/5 cups (360g) sugar
A little vinegar

1. Coarsely chop figs.

2. Put the figs from step 1, water, sugar and vinegar in a pan and heat. Crushing the figs at the beginning and mixing well, cook until the liquid is almost completely reduced and it becomes thick like jam.

Azuki-kan   P. 122

Red Bean Jelly
YIELDS AN 8.5"/21cm SQUARE CONTAINER

1.1lbs (500g) sweet red bean paste
1/3oz (10g) lemon zest (chopped finely)
2 Tablespoons lemon juice
1/3oz (10g) grated ginger
1 1/4 cups (300ml) water
0.4oz (12g) leaf gelatin (soaked in water)

1. Combine all the ingredients except gelatin in a pan, bring to a boil and turn off the heat.

2. Put the gelatin in the mixture from step 1 and let it dissolve. Pour the mixture into a container.

3. Let cool and refrigerate to harden. When it hardens, remove from the container and cut into serving pieces.

Hoji-cha Ice Cream   P. 122

Roasted Tea Ice Cream
YIELDS 3qts (3l)

2.5 quarts (2.5L) milk
1 1/2 cup (300g) granulated sugar
20 egg yolks
3 1/3oz (100g) *hoji-cha*, roasted tea

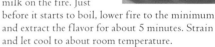

1. Put the roasted tea and milk on the fire. Just before it starts to boil, lower fire to the minimum and extract the flavor for about 5 minutes. Strain and let cool to about room temperature.

2. Combine the egg yolks and sugar and whisk well until the mixture turns pale and becomes thick. Slowly pour the milk tea from step 1 while mixing gently.

3. Put the mixture from step 2 into a pan and cook on low heat, constantly stirring and scraping the pan with a rubber spatula until the mixture reaches 180°F (82°C.) Do not boil or the yolks will curdle.

4. Strain the mixture from step 3, cool and freeze in an ice-cream maker.

Tanba-ji Matsukaze   P. 122

Black Soybean cake

5oz (150g) butter
4oz (120g) granulated sugar
5oz (150g) eggs
5.5oz (160g) pastry flour

0.4 teaspoon (5g) baking powder
1 1/2 Tablespoons milk
1/3oz (10g) honey
5.5oz (160g) *kuro-mame* (*ama-ni*), boiled black soybeans (sweetened)
5oz (150g) peeled chestnuts
1 3/4oz (50g) pine nuts
3 1/3oz (100g) raisins
3 1/3oz (100g) dried figs
Brandy as needed
Poppy seeds as needed
2 *yuzu*

1. Soften butter at a room temperature. Soak raisins and figs in brandy.

2. Cream granulated sugar with the butter from step 1.

3. Add beaten eggs gradually in six or seven stages to the mixture from step 2 and mix well.

4. Combine honey with the mixture from step 3, add milk and mix well.

5. Add sifted flour and baking powder, to step 4 mixture and mix roughly.

6. Combine the drained raisins and figs from step 1, pine nuts, black soybeans, chestnuts, and finely diced yuzu with the mixture from step 5 and mix well (if the ingredients to be combined are coated with 20g sifted flour, they combine more easily with the mixture).

7. Pour the mixture from step 6 into an 8.5"/21cm container and dent at the center and sprinkle with poppy seeds on its surface.

8. Bake it in a 350°F (180°C) oven for one hour.

9. When it is baked, place a glass plate on top to even the surface.

10. Cut into serving pieces.

WINTER

■ December *Hassun*

Tsubaki-zushi   P. 126

Camellia Sushi   SERVES 4

1 2/3oz (50g) smoked salmon
2 2/3oz (80g) sushi rice (see basic recipes)
1/2 egg yolk
A little *Tosa-zu* (see basic recipes)

1. Steam egg yolk and strain and add some Tosa-zu, warm the vessel containing the egg yolk in hot water and gently mix.

2. Cut smoked salmon into 1 3/4" (4cm) squares.

3. Divide sushi rice into 4 portions. Put a slice of smoked salmon on the sushi rice, form a round shape resembling a camellia using a moist towel. Place some cooked egg yolk at center of the "flower."

Ogawa Karasumi

Dried Mullet Roe Rolled with Squid

See January recipe

Sukeko

Cod Roe   SERVES 4

5 1/3oz (150g) *sukeko* fresh cod roe
0.4 cup (100ml) *dashi*
5 teaspoons sake
1 teaspoon light soy sauce
1 teaspoon *mirin*
A dash of salt
A little dried bonito flakes

1. Remove the veins of the cod roe and make a cut into the skin and turn it inside out. Blanch in boiling water until cooked. Plunge into ice water and when the water clears up, take the cod roe out and drain well.

2. Heat the cod roe from step 1, dashi and sake in a saucepan. Skim, season with light soy sauce, mirin and salt, and simmer covered with dried bonito flakes wrapped in gauze.

Nanohana Karashi-ae

Rapini with Japanese   SERVES 4
Mustard Dressing

12 *nanohana* rapini
Stock (10 Tablespoons *dashi*, 1/2 Tablespoon light soy sauce and a dash of salt)
1/2 teaspoon mixed Japanese mustard and western mustard

1. Blanch rapini in salted water until bright and cool in ice water. Drain well.

2. Bring stock to a boil and let to cool. Soak the rapini from step 1 in cool stock.

3. Dissolve the mixed mustard in the stock from step 2 and dress the rapini with it.

Namako Kokaku Kabu Mizore-ae

Sea Cucumber and Turnips   SERVES 4

1/2 sea cucumber
2/3oz (20g) Shogoin turnip
A little yuzu skin
1/2 Japanese chili pepper
3oz (100g) *daikon*
Sudachi juice to taste, slices for garnish
ban-cha coarse tea
Tosa-zu (see basic recipes) as needed

Tosa-zu jelly (7 Tablespoons Tosa-zu, 10 Tablespoons *dashi* and 1 teaspoon gelatin powder)

1. Make Tosa-zu jelly: put Tosa-zu, dashi in a pan on heat and add gelatin powder and dissolve. Refrigerate to harden and strain though a fine sieve.

2. Slice open the sea cucumber and rinse. Put it and 185°F (85°C) ban-cha tea in a heavy ceramic jar, with a lid and let cool.

3. Cut the sea cucumber from step 2 into serving pieces. Add yuzu skin and Japanese chili pepper to Tosa-zu and soak the sea cucumber in it for 1–2 hours.

4. Cut turnips into fine dice and soak in 2% salt water.

5. Grate daikon and squeeze out excess moisture and fluff.

6. Combine the sea cucumber from step 3, turnips from step 4, and grated daikon from step 5. Dress in Tosa-zu jelly and adjust the taste with sudachi juice.

---

7. Place a slice of sudachi on a plate and put the finished dish from step 6 and garnish with diced yuzu skin.

Karashi Renkon

Fried Lotus Root   SERVES 4
with Japanese Mustard

1/2 lotus root
2/3oz (20g) ground fish fillet
Stuffing: (2/3oz (20g) *Saikyo miso* paste, 1 teaspoon Japanese mustard and 1 teaspoon Dijon mustard)
A little dried bonito powder
Flour
Vegetable oil for deep-frying

1. Peel the lotus root. Soak in water, and steam.

2. Combine ground fish and stuffing in a food processor.

3. Powder the holes of lotus roots from step 1 with flour and fill them with the stuffing from step 2.

4. Coat the stuffed lotus root with flour and bonito powder. Deep-fry at about 320°F (160°C.)

5. Slice the fried lotus roots from step 4 into rounds.

February *Nimono-wan*
Suppon-goma-dofu Usu-gori-jitate   P. 129

Turtle Soup with Turnip "Ice"   SERVES 4

4 1/3oz (50g) *maru goma-dofu* sesame seed tofu (see below)
1/3 Shogoin turnip
2 *kuwai* a kind of water chestnut
1 3/4" (2cm) piece of red carrot
1 3/4" (2cm) piece of *daikon*
About 8cm of *Kujo negi* green onions (white part)
4 (3/4" (2cm) squares *kusa mochi*, rice cakes flavored with green mugwort
Ginger juice to taste
Gold leaf
Kuchinashi gardenias for yellow coloring
Happoji all-purpose *dashi* for turnips, *kuwai* and carrots (2 1/3 cups (540ml) dashi, 1 Tablespoon light soy sauce and 1/2 teaspoon salt)

Suppon snapping turtle soup
(2 cups (500ml) *dashi*, 2 cups (500ml) snapping turtle stock (see shark fin soup recipe p. 184) and 7 teaspoons light soy sauce)
Dissolved *kuzu* starch as needed

1. Pare turnips into a 4" (10cm) diameter cylindrical shape and cut into 1/25" (1mm) thick slices. Blanch in boiling water and soak in happoji.

2. Cut kuwai in halves and cut into the shape of a pentagonal votive tablet. Dye kuwai yellow in boiling water with kuchinashi and brand a seal of the appropriate Asian zodiac sign into it. Soak them in happoji.

3. Punch carrot and daikon pieces into blossom-shapes with a mold and slice. Simmer in happoji.

4. Sear Kujo negi onions until brown and cut into 3/4" (2cm) widths.

5. Bring snapping turtle soup to a boil and add the

onions from step 4 and simmer for 1–2 minutes. When the aroma and flavor of the onions transfers to the soup, take them out. Add ginger juice and thicken with dissolved kuzu.

6. Sear kusa mochi.

7. Place warmed suppon sesame seed tofu, onions, kuwai, and kusa mochi in a bowl and pour hot soup over them.

8. Bring the happoji from step 1 to a boil, drench the turnips in it and cover each bowl with a slice. Scatter with warmed blossom shaped carrots and daikon, and sprinkle with gold leaf.

Suppon **sesame seed tofu** (serves 4–5)

2 2/3oz (80g) snapping turtle meat (taken from soup and de-boned)
1oz (25g) kuzu (*Kumagawa hon-kuzu*)
Stock (1 1/4 cups (300ml) *dashi*, 1oz (35g) sesame seed paste, a little of light soy sauce and salt)

1. Finely chop turtle meat.

2. Stir kuzu into stock and mix well. Strain and put in a saucepan.

3. Put the pan on heat, stir for 15–20 minutes until the mixture thickens and add the meat. Take 1/4 of the mixture and wrap in wet gauze. Plunge into ice water and chill to harden. Repeat until you have 4 goma tofu balls.

■ January *Hassun*
Hanabira-zushi P. 130
Flower Petal Sushi SERVES 4

2oz (50g) smoked salmon
80g sushi rice (see basic recipes)
4 .2"×.2"×5" (5mm×5mm×13.5cm) piece of gobo root
4 .2"×.2"×5" (5mm×5mm×13.5cm) red carrots
Shogoin turnip as needed
Sweetened vinegar as needed

Mixed stock (3/4 cup (180ml) *dashi*, 1 teaspoon light soy sauce, pinch (1g) salt and 1/2 teaspoon *mirin*)

1. Cut smoked salmon into 4 thin slices about 3/4"×1 1/2" (2cm×4cm×3mm) wide.

2. Divide sushi rice into four portions, top with smoked salmon and make round pieces of sushi.

3. Simmer gobo and red carrots separately in mixed stock.

4. Cut turnips into a 6"×2" (14cm×5cm) cylindrical shape and slice into 1/12" (2mm) rounds. Soak in 3% solution of salty water for about 30 minutes and drain. Soak in sweetened vinegar.

5. Place one stick of gobo and carrot on the turnip slice from step 4 and fold in half to resemble a *hanabira mochi*.

Gomame Musubi
Dried Sardines SERVES 4

1oz (25g) *gomame* dried sardines
Stock (7 Tablespoons sake, 7 Tablespoons *mirin*, 5 teaspoons regular soy sauce and 1/2 teaspoon of *mizu-ame* millet syrup)

1. Place gomame on a heat-resistant plate and microwave for three minutes to dry.

2. Put stock ingredients in a pan, simmer until the liquid is reduced and caramelizes, add sardines and coat with the sauce, taking care not to burn.

Chishato Kasu-zuke
Chishato Pickled in Sake Lees SERVES 10

1 *chishato* a kind of lettuce stem
1lb (525g) *mirin kasu* mirin lees
10 Tablespoons *nikiri-zake*
2 Tablespoons light soy sauce
2 Tablespoons *mirin*

1. Cut chishato into 1 3/4" (3.5cm) lengths and peel the skin. Blanch in boiling salted water and cool on a rack.

2. Combine mirin lees, nikiri-zake, light soy sauce and mirin in a food processor and blend well.

3. Spread the half amount of the mixture from step 2 on tray and cover in gauze. Place the chishato on top and cover with gauze. Pour the rest of the mixture on top and pickle for about 12 hours.

Kuromame Matsuba-zashi
Black Soybeans Skewered on Pine Needles

7oz (200g) black soybeans
"A" syrup: 7oz (200g) sugar and 1qt (900ml) water)
"B" syrup: 14oz (400g) sugar and 1qt 900ml water)

1. Soak black soybeans in rice water with a little ash and a couple of rusty nails in a bowl overnight. Put the pan on low heat and simmer for about 1–2 days adding warm water (Ready when a bean thrown against a wall sticks to it).

2. Put beans in fresh water in a pan and bring to a boil. Repeat this process a few times. During the third time, heat the "A" syrup until it is the same temperature as the simmering liquid and gently transfer drained beans into the syrup. Simmer for a while and remove from the heat and let rest overnight.

3. Make "B" syrup and warm up it as same temperature to the same temperature as the "A" syrup and gently transfer beans.

4. Bring the pan with "B" syrup to a boil and turn down heat and gently simmer for about 15 minutes. Let cool. Skewer on pine needles.

Ogawa Karasumi
Dried Mullet Roe Rolled with Squid

5oz (140g) *karasumi* dried mullet roe
7oz (200g) *mongo ika* cuttlefish fillet
6oz (175g) *mirin kasu* mirin lees
Stock (2 teaspoons *nikiri-zake*, 1 teaspoon light soy sauce, 1 teaspoon regular soy sauce, 1/2 Tablespoon sugar and 1/2 teaspoon *mirin*)

1. Peel off the thin skin of the dried mullet roe.

2. Cut the squid fillet into a single 0.2" (5mm) thick piece.

3. Wrap the karasumi in squid and wrap it with gauze.

4. Combine mirin lees and stock and soak the karasumi roll in it for a couple of weeks in a refrigerator.

5. Take the karasumi roll out and slice into thin rounds.

Komochi Kombu
Kelp with Herring Roe SERVES 4

2oz (60g) *komochi kombu* kelp covered in herring roe
"A" stock (1 1/2 cups (360ml) *dashi*, 8 teaspoons light soy sauce and 8 teaspoons (40ml) *mirin*)
"B" stock (same as "A" stock)
1/3oz (10g) dried bonito flakes

1. Cut komochi konbu into 1"×1 3/4" (2.5cm×4.5cm) rectangles and soak in fresh water to remove salt.

2. Bring "A" stock in a pan to a boil and add the half of dried bonito flakes, turn off heat. When cooled, strain and soak the drained kombu from step 1 in it until the kombu absorbs some flavor.

3. Prepare "B" stock the same as "A." Remove kombu from "A" stock, drain and soak in cooled "B" stock.

Mame Kuwai
Small Water Chestnuts SERVES 4

8 *mame kuwai*, a kind of small water chestnuts
Kuchinashi Gardenia flowers for yellow color
Mixed stock (3/4 cups (170ml) *dashi*, 1 teaspoon light soy sauce, 1 teaspoon *mirin*, pinch of salt)

1. Pare mame kuwai into a hexagonal shape.

2. Chop kuchinashi, wrap in gauze, put in warm water and boil. Simmer the mame kuwai in the liquid briefly and when they are dyed yellow, cool them in fresh water.

3. Drain the kuwai and simmer in mixed stock and let cool.

December *Shiizakana Ebi-imo Nishu-age* P. 132
Fried Ebi-imo with Two Kinds of Crust SERVES 4

2 *Ebi-imo* a kind of taro root
Arare powder (finely crushed rice crackers): bake plain arare rice crackers in an oven until well browned and crush into pieces in a food processor; as needed
Flour slurry (2 Tablespoons flour, 6 Tablespoons water)
White poppy seeds as needed
1/3oz 10g Dried bonito flakes
Stock for simmering ebi-imo (1 3/4 (400ml) *dashi*, 2 Tablespoons light soy sauce, 8 teaspoons *mirin* and a dash of salt)
Vegetable oil for deep-frying
Yuzu skin (thinly sliced) to taste

1. Peel the ebi-imo and blanch them in rice-rinsing liquid. After plunging into water to cool, put them in a pan of fresh water and bring to a boil, remove ebi-imo.

2. Combine "A" stock and ebi-imo in a pan, bring

to a boil, cover the top with dried bonito flakes wrapped in gauze and simmer.

3. Cut the simmered ebi-imo into serving pieces and dredge in the slurry. Coat half the number of ebi imo in arare powder and the other half in poppy seeds, and deep-fry.

4. Arrange on a plate and top with yuzu skin.

December *Shiizakana*   *Kamo Nabe*   P. 132
Duck Hot Pot
SERVES 4

1 duck breast
4oz (120g) *Kujo negi* winter green onions
8 duck meatballs (see below)
Ground sansho pepper to taste

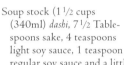
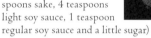

Soup stock (1 ½ cups (340ml) *dashi*, 7 ½ Tablespoons sake, 4 teaspoons light soy sauce, 1 teaspoon regular soy sauce and a little sugar)

1. Trim duck meat and remove sinews and extra fat. Slice the surface of the skin lengthwise every ¼" (7mm), do the same crosswise. Sauté the breast skin side down to render out excess fat. Let cool and cut into slices.

2. Cut Kujo negi on the diagonal.

3. Heat ingredients for soup stock.

4. Put ¼ portion of the stock from step 3 in an individual serving pot. Add the onions and duck meatballs and when they are heated, add the duck slices from step 1.

5. Dust with ground sansho pepper and serve immediately.

Duck meatballs (30 balls)

1lb (500g) ground duck meat
1oz (25g) ground fish fillet
3 ⅓ (100g) duck liver (steamed with sake and strained through a sieve)
½ egg yolk
½ egg
Dashi

1. Combine ground duck meat, ground fish, duck liver, egg yolk and egg in a food processor and pulse until smooth.

2. Divide the mixture into 30 portions and form into balls. Drop them in boiling dashi remove when cooked.

■ February *Hassun*

Tazuna-zushi   P. 134
Rein-Shaped Sushi
SERVES 8

2 sardines
2 *kuruma ebi* medium shrimp
5 *mitsuba* greens (stems only)
Pickling vinegar as needed (see basic recipes)
5 ⅓oz (150g) sushi rice (see basic recipes)
Kombu as needed

1. Fillet sardines, remove the belly bones and pin bones. Soak them in 4% salt water for one hour.

Towel dry and pickle by covering both sides with kombu.

2. Blanch the stems of mitsuba (discard leaves) until color turns brighter and cut into 3" (8cm) lengths.

3. Remove the heads of shrimps and devein. Skewer the abdomen side on bamboo sticks, cook them in boiling salted water.

4. When the shrimps are cooled, peel and slice lengthwise. Cut 3" (8cm) long slices and trim the edges. Quickly drench them in pickling vinegar and towel dry.

5. Cut 3" (8cm) slices of the sardines from step 1 and soak them in pickling vinegar for 5 minutes. Towel dry.

6. Make a stick shape out of sushi rice.

7. On a bamboo sushi mat, place the sardines, mitsuba, and shrimps parallel at about a 45 degree angle and top with the sushi rice stick from step 7. Roll and compress lightly to shape. Cut into 8 pieces.

Noshi Ume
Plum-Flower Jelly

Punch *noshi ume* (plum jelly) made by a local confectioner into the shape of a five-petaled plum flower with a mold.

Kuromame
Black Soybeans

See January recipe of *Kuromame Matsuba-zashi*.

Tara no Ko Rakugan
Cod Roe Cakes
YIELDS ABOUT 4lbs (1.8k)

2.2lbs (1k) *tarako* cod roe
1.1lbs (500g) *surimi* white meat fish paste
10 eggs
4 teaspoons *mirin*
5 teaspoons light soy souce
3 ⅓oz (100g) red carrots
200g lily bulbs
"A" stock (1 ½qts (1.5l) *dashi*, ½ cup (125ml) sake, 2 Tablespoons light soy sauce, 4 teaspoons *mirin* and a dash of salt)

"B" stock for simmering red carrots (1 ¼ cup (300ml) *dashi*, 2 Tablespoons light soy sauce and 1 Tablespoon *mirin*)

1. Rinse cod roe and make cuts into the surface. Put in boiling water and when they float to the surface, take out and plunge into ice water. Strain through a sieve to remove membrane and debris.

2. Drain the cod roe from step 1 and combine with "A" stock in a saucepan, simmer until the liquid is almost completely reduced.

3. Rinse lily bulbs and cut into bite-size pieces. Steam and lightly sprinkle with salt, then push through a sieve while still warm.

4. Cut red carrots into 1/12" (2mm) dice and simmer in stock "B."

---

5. Mix the cod roe, fish paste, eggs, mirin, soy sauce, lily bulb and carrots, put into a heatproof container and cook in a 195°F (90°C) oven for 90 minutes.

6. When cooled, remove cake from pan and cut into serving pieces.

Nanohana Karashi-ae
Rapini with Japanese Mustard Dressing

See December recipe

Ume Dofu
Plum Blossom Tofu
SERVES 24

1 cube of *momen* firm tofu
10-½oz (300g) red plum paste (jar)
1lb (450g) white plum paste (jar)
5 Tablespoons (75ml) *nikiri-zake*
2 Tablespoons (32.5ml) *mirin*

1. Put a heavy stone on tofu and leave for a half day to squeeze out excess water.

2. Combine red and white plum paste, nikiri-zake and mirin and marinate the tofu from step 1 for about a half day.

3. Punch tofu with a plum flower- shape mold.

Fuki no To Miso-zuke
Miso Pickled Fuki no To
SERVES 4

4 *fuki no to* coltsfoot buds
1lb (500g) Saikyo *miso* sweet white miso paste
5 Tablespoons (75ml) *nikiri-zake*
Vegetable oil for deep-frying
½ egg yolk for crumbles

1. Deep-fry fuki no to and pour boiling water over them to remove excess oil.

2. Add nikiri-zake to sweet white miso paste and mix well.

3. Place half amount of the miso mixture from step 2 on a tray and cover it with gauze. Add fuki no to from step 1 and cover with gauze again, pouring the rest of the miso mixture over it. Cure fuki no to in the mixture for a half day.

4. Steam egg yolk and strain through a fine sieve, keep in a warm bowl. Remove the fuki no to from the miso mixture and cover in crumbled egg yolk.

Shirauo Yuzuka-ni
Cooked Whitebait with Yuzu

½lb (250g) fresh whitebait
⅓oz (10g) yuzu skin
"A" stock (10 Tablespoons sake, ½ teaspoon salt, ½ teaspoon light soy sauce and ½ teaspoon *mirin*)

1. Rinse whitebait quickly to remove debris.

2. Drain the whitebait from step 1 and put in a pan with yuzu skin and "A" stock. Simmer until the liquid is almost completely reduced. Let cool.

Hanawasabi
Japanese Horseradish Blossoms

1oz (30g) wasabi blossoms
Mixed stock (¾ cups (180ml) *dashi*, 2 teaspoons light soy sauce, dash of salt)

1. Bring mixed stock to a boil and let cool. When cool, chill the vessel containing mixed stock in ice water.

2. Blanch wasabi blossoms in salted water and drain. Immediately plunge them into the chilled mixed stock from step 1.

3. Remove and cut into about ³/₄" (2cm) lengths.

February *Yakimono* **Managatsuo Nanban-yaki** P. 136

Pompano Grilled Nanban Style SERVES 4

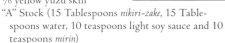

10oz (280g) Pompano fillet cut in four pieces

Marinade
1 ¹/₃oz (40g) *Kujo negi* winter green onions (chopped)
1 small Japanese chili pepper
²/₃oz (20g) ginger (sliced)
¹/₆ yellow yuzu skin
"A" Stock (15 Tablespoons *nikiri-zake*, 15 Tablespoons water, 10 teaspoons light soy sauce and 10 teaspoons *mirin*)

Topping
1 ¹/₂oz (45g) *Kujo negi* green onions
1oz (30g) gingers
¹/₆ Yellow yuzu skin
"B" stock (2 Tablespoons *nikiri-zake*, 2 Tablespoons water, 2 teaspoons light soy sauce 2 teaspoons *mirin*)

1. Make cuts into the pompano skin.

2. Mix the marinade and macerate the pompano from step 1 for 12 hours.

3. Chop onions, ginger, and yellow yuzu skin for topping into fine pieces. Combine them with "B" stock and soak until the topping absorbs some flavor from the stock, drain.

4. Skewer the pompano from step 1, folding edges and broil. Sprinkle with the toppings from step 3 and quickly sear with a butane torch.

Hotate kaibashira karasumi-ko yaki
Baked scallops dusted with karasumi (serves 4)

4 Sea scallops
1oz (30g) *karasumi* dried mullet roe
¹/₂ egg yolk
A dash of salt

1. Make karasumi crumbs: Remove the thin membrane of the karasumi and grate it with an *oroshigane* Japanese grater.

2. Warm the grated karasumi from step 1 with hot water and dry.

3. Lightly sprinkle scallops with salt and skewer. Broil until almost cooked. Paint with egg yolk, coat the top side with the karasumi crumbs and lightly broil.

Amigasa yuzu

1 yuzu
Lime (limestone), a little
⁴/₅ cup (200ml) water
¹/₂ cup (100g) sugar

1. Grate off the outer skin of yuzu with and reserve for another use.

2. Cut yuzu in half lengthwise, scoop out the pulp leaving only the pith, then blanch in boiling water with some lime. Plunge into ice water and remove any inside strings.

3. Blanch the yuzu pith in fresh water again and plunge into cool water. Put the yuzu in a bamboo sieve and steam for about 10 minutes.

4. Combine water, sugar and the yuzu from step 3 and simmer until the liquid is almost completely reduced and glossy. Cool and slice into 1 ¹/₂" (3cm) long strips for garnish.

February *Gohan* **Anago Ii-mushi** P. 138

Sea Eel with Rice SERVES 4

5 sea eels (really small ones)
14oz (400g) *Shiro-mushi*: just steamed *mochi-gome* glutinous rice (without any seasoning)
Chorogi (see below)
kinome leaf buds to taste
"A" stock for sea eel (2 cups (450ml) sake, 2 cups water (450ml) water, 10 Tablespoons regular soy sauce, 10 Tablespoons *mirin* and a little sugar)
"B" stock for sauce (7 Tablespoons sea eel cooking liquid, 7 Tablespoons sake, 2 teaspoons mizu ame millet syrup and 1 teaspoon regular soy sauce)

1. Fillet sea eels and place on a cutting board meat side down. Cover skin with towel and pour boiling water over the fillets and quickly plunge into ice water.

2. Combine "A" stock and eels from step 1 and simmer gently. When cooked, remove eels and let cool, reserve cooking liquid. Chop one sea eel into fine pieces.

3. Combine "B" stock in a pan and simmer until the liquid is reduced to a light syrup.

4. Pour ¹/₃ cup (70ml) cooking liquid from step 2 over the steamed glutinous rice, add chopped eel from step 2, mix roughly and divide into 4 portions.

5. Wrap the rice from step 4 in the sea eel from step 2 and brush the surface of the sea eel with the sauce from step 3. Steam until heated through, then garnish with kinome leaf buds.

Chorogi

Chorogi a small root vegetable known as Japanese artichoke.
Sweetened vinegar (see basic recipes)

1. Boil chorogi and leave to cool on a rack.

2. Soak the chorogi from step 1 in sweetened vinegar.

3. Skewer with pine needles.

December *Sakizuke*
Kumiage Yuba Konowata-mushi P. 140

Kumiage Yuba and SERVES 4
Sea Cucumber Roe

³/₄lb (350g) *Kumiage yuba* soft fresh soy-milk skin
Ground sesame seeds (see basic recipes)

³/₄ cup (180ml) dashi
1 teaspoon light soy sauce
A dash of salt
2 teaspoons *konowata* salted sea cucumber entrails
Konoko dried sea cucumber ovaries

1. Combine kumiage yuba and ground sesame seeds in a food processor and blend well. Dilute with dashi and season with light soy sauce and salt.

2. Sear the surface of konoko and finely dice.

3. Chop konowata roughly with a knife.

4. Combine the konowata and kumiage yuba from step 1 into a bowl, cover and steam until heated through.

5. When done, top with the konoko.

February *Sakizuke* **Kinko-mushi** P. 140

Steamed Sea Cucumber SERVES 8

1 *kinko* dried sea cucumber
²/₃oz (20ml) *konowata*
Chives (chopped) as needed
Ginger juice as needed
"A" stock for kinko (10 Tablespoons *dashi*, 2 Tablespoons sake, 1 Tablespoon light soy sauce, 1 teaspoon *mirin*)
"B" stock for *gin-an* silver sauce (1 ³/₄ cups (400ml) *dashi*, 2 teaspoons light soy sauce, ¹/₂ teaspoon salt and 1 teaspoon *mirin*)
Dissolved *kuzu* starch as needed

1. Soak kinko in rice rinsing water for 1 day.

2. Steam the kinko in the soaking liquid for 30 minutes. Let cool and repeat the process.

3. Cut open the abdomen side of kinko and remove entrails.

4. Put the kinko from step 3 into a container of fresh water and steam for about 30 minutes, remove and let cool. Repeat the process until the kinko is tender.

5. When the kinko is tender, simmer in "A" stock. Cut into small pieces.

6. Make gin-an silver sauce: Bring "B" stock in a pan to a boil and thicken with dissolved kuzu.

7. Place the kinko from step 5 in 8 small bowls and add a little chopped konowata. Pour in silver sauce, seal with plastic film and steam until cooked. Add ginger juice and garnish with chopped chives.

January *Sakizuke* **Sekihan-mushi** P. 140

Red Rice SERVES 4

4 ¹/₄oz (120g) *sekihan* steamed glutinous rice with red beans
Salted Nihon-*shu* (2 Tablespoons sake and a dash of salt)
¹/₂ cup (120ml) *kumiage yuba* fresh soy-milk skin
4 *uguisuna* small turnips
"A" stock (1 ¹/₄ cups (180ml) *dashi*, 1 teaspoon light soy sauce and a pinch of salt)
Fresh sea urchin roe
Grated wasabi

Bekko an amber sauce

"B" stock (9 1/2 Tablespoons *dashi*, 2 teaspoons regular soy sauce, 1/2 Tablespoon *mirin*)
Dissolved kuzu as needed

1. Peel the uguisuna and cook in boiling water and soak in "A" stock.

2. Steam red rice and drizzle with boiled sake and salt. Mix well and divide into 4 portions.

3. Put the cooked red rice in a small bowl and lightly steam. When it is done, top with kumiage yuba and steam a bit more. Then top with fresh sea urchin roe and the uguisuna from step 1 and steam until heated.

4. Bring "B" stock for bekko an to a boil and thicken with dissolved kuzu. Pour the sauce over the rice from step 3 and garnish with grated wasabi.

■ Winter *Mukozuke*

Okoze　　　　　　　　　　　　　　P. 142

Scorpion Fish

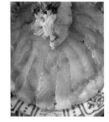

Okoze scorpion fish
Pon-zu citrus vinegar (see basic recipes)
Scallions
Momiji oroshi grated daikon and Japanese chili pepper to taste

1. Rinse scorpion fish and carefully slice along both sides of the poisonous dorsal fin. Remove fin by holding it down with a heavy knife and tearing the fish away from it. Fillet and pick out pin bones with tweezers, peel the skin and reserve with the liver and stomach.

2. Blanch the skin and stomach in boiling water and plunge into ice water. Towel dry and cut into fine pieces. Blanch the liver and plunge into ice water, and then towel dry and cut into serving pieces.

3. Slice the fillet into thin pieces, arrange on a plate and put the liver, skin and stomach to the side. Serve with pon-zu, chopped scallions and momiji oroshi.

Ise Ebi　　　　　　　　　　　　　P. 144

Spiny Lobster

Ise ebi spiny lobster
Tosa soy sauce (see basic recipes)
Grated *wasabi*

1. Remove the head, make a cut on each side of the shell on the abdomen and remove the thin shell. Scoop out the meat with a spoon.

2. Cut the meat into halves lengthwise and remove the intestine. Cut each half in two and rinse in ice water to remove blood and firm up the meat.

3. Towel dry and cut into serving pieces. Serve with Tosa soy sauce and grated wasabi.

Maguro Toro　　　　　　　　　　　P. 144

Fatty Tuna

Hon maguro tuna

Tosa soy sauce
4 egg yolks
Dissolved Japanese mustard

1. For egg yolk soy sauce: Soak unbroken egg yolks in Tosa soy sauce for about 1–2 days, whisk well to finish sauce.

2. Fillet tuna into blocks and slice into serving pieces. Serve with prepared Japanese mustard and egg yolk soy sauce.

January *Yakimono*　*Managatsuo Hosho-yaki*　P. 146

Papillote of Pompano　　　　　SERVES 10

1lb (500g) pompano fillet cut in 10 pieces
Miso yuanji miso paste as needed (See basic recipes)

1. Make slices in the skin of the pompano pieces.

2. Cure the pompano from step 1 in miso yuanji for 12 hours.

3. Take the pompano out of the miso paste from step 2 and sear the skin side with a butane torch until browned, without cooking the inside.

4. Wrap the pompano from step 3 in wet *hosho* paper, and bake in a 350°F (180°C) oven for 10 minutes.

5. Tie the paper from step 4 with *mizuhiki* red and white strings and arrange on a plate.

Yaki hamaguri　Grilled Clams

10 clams
Egg whites as needed
Salt as needed

1. Break clams' hinge joint so they don't open when heated.

2. Cover the clams with egg whites and coat with salt. Bake in a 300°F (150°C) oven for about 10 minutes.

Kinkan-ni　Simmered kumquats

10 kumquats
Syrup (14 Tablespoons (170g) sugar and 2 cups (450ml) water)

1. Cut kumquats in half and boil. Plunge into cold water and remove the seeds.

2. Drain and steam kumquats for about 10 minutes and dry them.

3. When the kumquats from step 2 are cooled, simmer them in syrup.

January *Shiizakana*　*Fukahire Nabe*　P. 148

Shark Fin Hot Pot

4 shark fins (each piece weighs about 80g)
Suppon snapping turtle meat (from turtle carcass used for stock) as needed
Kujo negi 1"×3" (3cm×8cm) piece of winter green onion (white part only)
8 pieces of sesame seed tofu (see below)

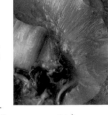

"A" stock for simmering shark fins (2 1/2 cups (600ml) *dashi*, 10 Tablespoons snapping turtle soup (see below) and 4 1/2 teaspoons light soy sauce)
"B" stock for soup (1 cup (250ml) *dashi*, 1 cup (250ml) snapping turtle soup (see below), 1 Tablespoon light soy sauce and 1 teaspoon *mirin*)
Dissolved kuzu as needed
Ginger juice to taste

1. Blanch shark fins in boiling water and plunge into cool water and drain well.

2. Combine the shark fins from step 1 and "A" stock in a pan and simmer for about 20–25 minutes. Let cool in the stock.

3. Skewer and grill onions until well browned.

4. Bring "B" stock to a boil and lightly thicken with dissolved kuzu.

5. Pour a portion of the soup for each person in an individual serving pot, arrange the turtle meat, shark's fin, grilled onions and sesame seed tofu and simmer gently. To serve, season with a substantial amount of ginger juice.

Snapping turtle soup

6lbs (5kg) *suppon* snapping turtles
10qts (9l) water
2 3/4qts (2.7l) sake
1/2lb (250g) ginger

1. Dress snapping turtles, drench in boiling water and peel off the thin skin. Quickly rinse, combine with water, sake and small chunks of ginger and gently simmer for about 1 1/2 to 2 hours, skimming any scum that rises to the surface.

2. When the soup stock is full flavored, remove the meat and bones and strain.

Sesame seed tofu (for a 8.5" (21cm) square container)

6 cups (1.4l) *dashi*
6oz (180g) sesame seed paste
5oz (150g) kuzu (*Kumagawa hon-kuzu*)
2 teaspoons light soy sauce
A pinch of salt

1. Combine sesame seed paste and kuzu, add dashi and mix well. Strain through a fine sieve.

2. Put the mixture from step 1 into a saucepan, heat and stir about for 20 minutes. When the mixture thickens, adjust the taste with light soy sauce and salt.

3. Transfer the mixture to an 8.5" square container, cover and place the container in ice water to cool. When cooled and hardened, cut into serving pieces.

December *Futamono*　*Kabura-mushi*　P. 148

Steamed Turnips　　　　　　　SERVES 4

1 1/4lbs (560g) Shogoin turnips
4 1 3/4oz (50g) pieces of *guji* tilefish fillet
1/30oz (1g) dried kikurage cloud ear mushrooms
2oz (60g) lily bulbs
1/2 bunch of *mitsuba*

8 *ginnan* ginkgo nuts
1/4 box fresh sea urchin roe
1 egg white
A dash of salt
Light soy sauce to taste
"A" stock for cloud ear
mushrooms (6 Table-
spoons *dashi*, 1/2 teaspoon
light soy sauce and dash
of salt)
"B" stock *gin-an* silver sauce (1 3/4 cups (400ml)
dashi, 2 teaspoons light soy sauce, 1/2 teaspoon salt
and 1 teaspoon *mirin*)
Dissolved *kuzu* as needed
Grated *wasabi* to taste
Hari nori thinly sliced dried seaweed to taste

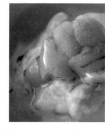

1. Lightly sprinkle tilefish with salt and leave for a
   while.

2. Blanch the tilefish from step 1

3. Soak cloud ear mushrooms in water and cut into
   thin slices. After quickly blanching them, soak in
   stock "A" that has been boiled and cooled.

4. Shell and peel ginkgo nuts. Blanch them in boiling water, lightly sprinkle with salt and cut into
   halves.

5. Rinse lily bulbs and cut into serving pieces and
   steam with salt.

6. Cut only stems of mitsuba into 3/4"/1.5cm lengths
   (discard leaves).

7. Peel turnips, grate and drain them in a sieve for
   5–10 minutes. Gently season them with light soy
   sauce and salt and combine with the ear cloud
   mushrooms, ginkgo nuts, lily bulbs, mitsuba and
   an egg white beaten to a stiff meringue. Gently
   mix.

8. Put the tilefish in a bowl and steam for 8–9 minutes. Cover it with the mixture from step 7 and
   steam for 4–5 minutes more.

9. Top the bowl from step 8 with fresh sea urchin
   roe and quickly steam.

10. Bring "B" stock to a boil and thicken with dis-
    solved kuzu to make silver sauce. Sauce the bowl
    from step 9 with the silver sauce and garnish
    with grated wasabi. Not pictured but you might
    want to garnish with some hari nori to taste.

Grilled Snow Crabs

Matsuba gani Snow crab

1. Prepare snow crabs. Cut
   off the legs and remove
   half of the shell with a
   knife.

2. Grill over charcoal. When
   the meat swells, it is ready
   to serve.

Squid and Scallions
with Miso Dressing   SERVES 4

1/3 cube *Omi konnyaku* red colored devil's tongue jelly
2 bunches of *wakegi* scallions
3 1/3oz (100g) squid (rinsed and prepared)

1/3 *daidai* sour orange for
juice and *chinpi*; dried and
sliced daidai skin
"A" mixed stock for sim-
mering konnyaku (3/4 cup
(180ml) *dashi*, 1 Table-
spoon light soy sauce 1
teaspoon *mirin*)
Seasoning for squid (1
Tablespoon sake and a
dash of salt)
2 2/3oz (80g) miso and vinegar dressing (see below)
Dissolved Japanese mustard to taste

1. Make chinpi: Peel the skin of daidai and dry it on
   a rack in the shade for about a day. Squeeze the
   juice and reserve. When the skin is dry, cut into
   fine slices.

2. Cut konnyaku into 1 1/2" (3cm) length sticks.
   Blanch in boiling water and then simmer in "A"
   mixed stock until reduced.

3. Cut squid the same size as the konnyaku and broil
   with salted sake.

4. Cut off the roots of wakegi scallions and bundle
   them at the bottom with cooking string, blanch
   and plunge into ice water. Towel dry on a cutting
   board to remove any sliminess. Cut into 1 1/2"
   (3cm) lengths.

5. Combine the drained konnyaku from step 2,
   the squid from 3 and the scallions from step 4,
   adjusting the taste with miso and vinegar dressing, dissolved Japanese mustard and the daidai
   juice from step 1 and mix well.

6. Place some of the mixture from step 5 on a plate
   and top with the chinpi daidai skin.

Miso and vinegar dressing

5oz (150g) white miso paste
5 Tablespoons (75ml) sake
1/2 egg yolk
4 teaspoons (20ml) vinegar
2 1/2 Tablespoons sugar

1. Combine white miso paste and sake in pan. Put
   the pan on medium heat and when it boils turn
   heat to low. Taking care not to burn, stir and
   simmer for about 10 minutes until it becomes as
   thick as the original miso paste.

2. When the paste from step 1 is cooled, add sugar,
   egg yolk, and vinegar and mix well.

Lily Bulb Dumplings   SERVES ABOUT 10

Quail filling
1/2 lb (250g) minced quail
meat
"A" stock (1 3/4 cups
(400ml) sake, 2 teaspoons
regular soy sauce, 3/4 teaspoon light soy sauce and
1 teaspoon *mirin*)
1oz (30g) *foie gras*
Ground *sansho* pepper to
taste

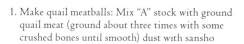

1. Make quail meatballs: Mix "A" stock with ground
   quail meat (ground about three times with some
   crushed bones until smooth) dust with sansho

---

powder and simmer until done. Let cool and combine with foie gras in a food processor. Shape into
2/3oz meatballs (20g).

Lily bulb mixture

10-1/2 (300g) *Yurine* raw lily bulbs (rinsed)
3oz (100g) *yamaimo* mountain yams (grated)
1oz (35g) rice-flour for dumplings
nikiri-zake as needed
1 egg white
1/5 cup (50ml) fresh cream
Light soy sauce to taste
Salt to taste

1. Rinse lily bulbs and cut into pieces for steaming.
   Steam and while still warm, strain through a fine
   sieve and let cool.

2. Mix rice-flour with nikiri-zake and make a dough
   about as soft as an ear lobe.

3. Put the lily bulbs from step 1, yams, the dough
   from step 2, egg white, and fresh cream in a food
   processor and blend well. Season with salt and
   light soy sauce, let the dough rest in the refrigerator.

4. When dough is rested, wrap the quail meatballs in
   the 1 1/3oz (40g) pieces of dough for each dumpling.

10 *aomi daikon* green radishes
1/2 red carrot
"B" stock (2 1/2 cups (360ml) *dashi*, 2 teaspoons light
soy sauce and 1/3 teaspoon salt)

Cut green radishes into thin strips. Cut red carrot
the same as the green radishes. Sprinkle both of
them with salt and when they become flexible,
place one carrot ribbon and one radish ribbon
together and tie into a knot. Rinse salt, blanch
quickly in boiling water and plunge into cool
water. Drain well and soak in "B" stock that has
been boiled once.

Kinome an leaf bud sauce

"C" stock (1qt (1l) *dashi* 5 teaspoons light soy sauce
and 1 teaspoon salt)
Dissolved kuzu as needed
1/6oz (5–6g) *kinome* leaf buds

1. Bring "C" stock to a boil in a saucepan and
   thicken with dissolved *kuzu* starch. Add chopped
   kinome leaf buds and mix.

To serve: Steam the lily bulb dumplings and garnish
with the tied radish and carrot strings and nap
with the leaf bud sauce.

Snowy Hot Pot   SERVES 4

4 20z (60g) *Guji* tilefish
fillet
1/2 bunch of *kikuna* edible
chrysanthemum leaves
8 1" (2.5cm) cubes of tofu
1/2 *daikon* giant radish
Boiled *fuki no to* coltsfoot
buds
Arare yuzu diced yuzu to
taste
Grated yuzu

"A" stock for soaking chrysanthemum leaves (1½ cups ((360ml) *dashi*, 2 teaspoons light soy sauce, dash of salt)
"B" stock (2¼ cups (540ml) *dashi*, 1 Tablespoon light soy sauce and ½ teaspoon salt)

1. Quickly blanch tilefish. Drain and cut each piece into 5 slices.

2. Pick leaves from chrysanthemum (no stems), and quickly blanch in boiling water and plunge into cold water. Drain well. Soak in "A" stock that has been boiled and cooled.

3. Peel the daikon and grate on an *oroshi-gane* Japanese grater. Let drain naturally in a fine sieve.

4. Bring "B" stock to a boil in a saucepan.

5. Pour individual portions of the soup from step 4 in small serving pots. Arrange the tilefish from step 1 and the tofu cubes and put the pot on heat. When the tilefish is cooked, add the chrysanthemum leaves and top with the drained, grated daikon. Garnish with fuki no to, diced yuzu and grated yuzu.

■ Winter *Mizumono*

Kinkan Sorbet   P. 159

Kumquat Sorbet   SERVES 20

1qt (1l) yogurt
Zest of 6 *kinkan* kumquats
2½oz (75g) *nishi ume* plum jelly
6¾ Tablespoons (100ml) kumquat syrup (whole kumquats simmered in 200ml water and ⅘ cup

(160g) sugar for 2 hours and filtered)
3⅓oz (100g) sugar
A drizzling of Cointreau orange liqueur

1. Finely dice the kumquat zest and plum jelly. Combine them with kumquat syrup.

2. Add sugar, the mixture from step 1 and cointreau to yogurt and mix.

3. Freeze the mixture from step 2 in an ice-cream maker.

Fruit Jelly   P. 159

Fruit Jelly

(for an 8.5" (21cm) square container)

½lb (250g) strawberries
½lb (250g) kiwi fruits
10½oz (300g) oranges
1¾ cups (400ml) water
2¾ Tablespoons (40ml) of *keihua jiu* Chinese osmanthus flower liqueur
6½ Tablespoons (80g) sugar
1oz (35g) pearl agar seaweed gelling agent, available at Japanese grocers

1. Remove stems from strawberries. Pare Kiwi fruit and scoop out the light core. Peel oranges. Cut into small pieces. Arrange evenly in the 8.5" container.

2. Combine water, sugar and pearl agar, bring to a boil. Add osmanthus liqueur and cool to 158°F (70°C.)

3. Pour the mixture over the fruit in the container and cover it with a glass board. Cool the container in ice water. When cooled, cut into serving pieces.

Yuki-mochi Matsu   P. 159

Snowy Dumplings   SERVES 14

½ cup (70g) rice-flour
½ cup (100g) sugar
1⅔oz (50g) *yamaimo* mountain yams
5oz (150g) sweet white bean paste
Green food coloring
Vinegar as needed
Pine nuts as needed

1. Sift together rice-flour and sugar.

2. Add green food color to sweet bean paste to make light green paste.

3. Grind yams smooth with a Japanese mortar and pestle, mix in flour and sugar little by little to make dough for wrapping the bean paste. Take ½oz (15g) dough and wrap 1⅓oz (10g) paste from step 2 into a dome shaped dumplings.

4. Spray dumplings with water and vinegar (water: vinegar=10:1) and steam. Garnish with pine nuts.

GLOSSARY

A

Aouri: Green gourd related to melons and cucumbers. (*Cucumis melo*).

Amadai: See guji

An: A thickened sauce, usually made with dissolved kuzu starch.

Awabi: Abalone (*Haliotis sorenseni*) a luxury shellfish with crisp textured meat. Usually eaten raw, steamed with sake or grilled.

Ayu: Sweetfish (*Plecoglossus altivelis altivelis*) caught in rivers but it actually spends half of its life in the sea. Its sides are blue and olive colored and its abdomen is silver white.

C

Chorogi: (*Stachys affinis*) a small root vegetable known as Japanese artichoke. When boiled, it is similar in taste and texture to *yurine*, lily bulbs. It is often dyed red at the New Year.

D

Daikon: Japanese white radish. (*Raphanus sativus*) When boiled it has a plain taste, but is sharper when grated raw and used as a garnish for dipping sauces. Often dried or pickled.

Dashi: Ubiquitous Japanese stock made of kombu and dried bonito flakes. Small dried sardines or *shiitake* mushrooms are sometimes added as well.

Dobo-zuke: A kind of pickle called dobo-zuke in Kyoto, but more widely known as *nuka-zuke*, made by curing vegetables in *nuka* (rice bran).

Dojo: Loaches (*Misgurnus anguillicaudatus*) found in swampy areas and drainage ditches.

E

Ebi: A general term for a shrimp or prawns.

Ebi-imo: A kind of taro root. Its shape and striped coloring resembles a shrimp.

F

Fu: Wheat gluten. It is often eaten in miso soup.

Fuki no to: Coltsfoot buds (*Petasites japonicus*) its stalks, known as *fuki*, are usually simmered. Both are essential spring vegetables.

G

Ginnan: Ginkgo nuts from the "living fossil" tree, *Ginkgo biloba*. A symbol of autumn.

Glutamic acids: A group of flavor enhancing amino acids considered to contribute to an *umami* taste. Foodstuffs rich in glutamic acid include cheese, green tea, bonito, kombu (kelp), and mushrooms.

Guji: A tilefish. Called *"guji"* in western Japan, this white fleshed snapper-like fish is is known as *amadai* in other regions (*Branchiostegus japonicus*).

H

Haccho miso: A robustly flavored, dark red fermented soybean paste. The most famous example is produced in Okazaki, Aichi prefecture.

Hajikami: Ginger stalks (*Zingiber officinale*) Pickled in vinegar and usually served as a garnish for grilled fish.

Hamo: A favorite Kyoto fish often translated as pike conger (*Muraenesox cinereus*) A sharp toothed eel-like fish with many small bones.

Hamokiri bocho: Special heavy knife for slicing through tiny bones of hamo.

Hari nori: Finely sliced dried *nori* seaweed.

Hatakena: A type of Kyoto mustard greens.

Heian period (794–1185): By this time, the basic way of Japanese cooking and cultural customs had been established. Nobles enjoyed a luxurious life style while the common folk were poor.

Hirame: a left-eyed flat fish (*Paralichthys olivaceus*) often translated as halibut.

Hikiage yuba: A sheet of soybean skin, can be fresh or dried.

Hirosu: A mixture of tofu, grated *tsukune imo* tsukune yam, chopped carrots, cloud ear mushrooms, ginkgo nuts and so forth rolled into balls and deep-fried. More commonly known as *gan-modoki* or mock goose.

I

Iidako: Roe filled tiny octopus (*Octopus ocellatus*) since they have many eggs that look like rice grains, they are called ii dako. Ii means rice in Japanese.

Ito hana katsuo: Finely sliced dried bonito flakes used as a garnish.

K

Kabosu: A spherical green citrus fruit (*Citrus sphaerocarpa*) with a strong and refreshing flavor, often used to garnish fish dishes.

Kamasu: Barracuda (*Sphyraena barracuda*.)

Kamo: Duck, famously paired with Japanese onions.

Kanten: A hardening agent made of agar seaweed (*Gelidium crinale*)

Katsuo: Bonito (*Katsuwonus pelamis*) usually eaten as sashimi or filleted, dried and thinly shaved to make dashi.

Katsuobushi: Dried bonito flakes.

Katsura muki: A knife technique used to peel a single sheet from a cylindrical shaped piece of vegetable, usually cucumber, daikon or carrot.

Kikuna, shungiku: Edible chrysanthemum leaves (*Chrysanthemum coronarium*) called kikuna in fall, shungiku in spring.

Kinugoshi tofu: A soft and delicate tofu, its name means "strained through silk."

Kinome
The tender leaf buds of the Japanese pepper tree (*Zanthoxylum piperitum*).

Kintoki ninjin: Kyoto red carrots, often called *kyo-ninjin*.

Kogomi: An edible fiddlehead fern (*Matteucciastruthiopteris*) a common spring ingredient.

Koji: Steamed rice which has been inoculated with *koji* mold spores (*Aspergillus Oryzae*) The mold produces enzymes that convert the starches in the rice into fermentable sugars for sake brewing.

Kombu: Kelp, a kind of seaweed (*Laminaria japonica*) contains substantial amounts of glutamic acids. Used for making stock for many kinds of dishes in Japanese cooking.

Konowata: Fermented sea cucumber entrails.

Konoko: Dried sea cucumber roe ovaries.

Kujo negi: A kind of winter green onion. Kujo is the name of a district of Kyoto.

Kumiage yuba: A creamy fresh soy-milk skin.

Kuruma ebi: A medium size shrimp (*Penaeus japonicus*) an important ingredient in Japanese cooking.

Kyo yasai: A general term for Kyoto's local vegetables. For example, kintoki ninjin, Shogoin turnips, Kujo negi green onions, kamo nasu eggplants and so on.

M

Matsuba-gani: Male snow crabs, *zuwai-gani*, (*Chionoecetes opilio*) since the male crabs are so different from female in size and taste, they are called by a different name.

Mibuna: A type of Kyoto greens, similar to mizuna.

Migaki nishin: Dried herring. An everyday food in Kyoto.

Miso: A salty fermented soybean paste, one of the most important seasonings in Japanese cooking

Mizuna: Pot herb mustard, a kind of Kyoto greens (*Brassica rapa*). It is called "kyo-na" as well. It has a light flavor and crisp texture, and is used for dressed dishes, salad, hot pots, simmered dishes and so on.

Momen dofu: A kind of tofu whose texture is firmer than silken tofu. It is used for simmered dishes.

Mukago: Nut-like propagulum, especially of yams.

Myoga: A Japanese ginger blossom (*Zingiber mioga*) due to its strong fragrance, it is often used raw to garnish miso soup or simmered dishes.

N

Nagaimo: Chinese yam (*Discorea opposita*) a long yam with a slimy texture, most often eaten raw.

Na no hana, nabana: Rape blossoms or rapini. (*Brassica campestris*) often cooked for dressed dishes. It is a symbol of spring in Japanese cooking.

Nasu: Japanese eggplants (*Solanum melongena*) usually slim and long but there are a number of other kinds.

Ni-ban dashi: A second stock made from dried bonito flakes and *kombu* that have been used once to make *ichiban-dashi* (first stock).

Nigari: Magnesium salts used as a coagulating agent for soy milk to make tofu. Made from sea water.

Nikiri-zake: Sake has which has its alcohol cooked off. It is used to dilute salty liquids or miso paste.

Nuka: Rice bran. It is used for pickling vegetables. In Kyoto the technique is called dobo-zuke.

O

Okoze: Scorpion fish (*Inimicus japonicus*) So named because of its poisonous dorsal spines.

Otsukuri: A sashimi dish. The word means the creation of a dish by slicing.

P

Pon-zu: Citrus-flavored vinegar. See basic recipes.

R

Rikyu-fu: A kind of simmered wheat gluten seasoned with regular soy sauce.

S

Saba: Mackerel (*Scomber australasicus*) its body is silver blue. They are commonly eaten as raw or pickled sashimi, in grilled dishes or simmered in miso paste.

Saikyo miso: A sweet white fermented soybean paste. It is a major seasoning in Kyoto cuisine. Saikyo means west Kyoto.

Sake: Rice wine, a popular beverage also used in Japanese cooking.

Sakura miso: A sweet mild red miso paste popular in Western Japan

Salamander: A restaurant broiler used for browning the surface of fish, meat or vegetables.

Sansho: Japanese pepper (*Zanthoxylum piperitum*) The leaf buds of the plant are called *kinome*.

Shichirin: An individual ceramic charcoal stove used for cooking and heating at home in winter.

Shima aji: Yellow jack (*Pseudocaranx dentex*)

Shime saba: Mackerel lightly pickled in vinegar and salt.

Shiroita kombu: A thin sheet of kombu.

Shiso: A fragrant herb (*Perilla frutescens*) often translated as "beefsteak leaf."

Soba: Buckwheat or buckwheat noodles

Sudachi: A kind of tart citrus fruit (*Citrus sudachi*) it is used to garnish many dishes. Picked green, it turns yellow.

Suribachi: A ceramic mortar bowl with a corrugated interior used for grinding ingredients. *Surikogi* is a wooden pestle used with the suribachi.

T

Tade: Water pepper (*Persicaria hydropiper*) an herb used to provide a spicy heat.

Tade-zu: Ground tade diluted with vinegar. It is served with grilled *ayu*.

Togan: Winter melon, a kind of melon that is not sweet, used for simmered dishes.

Tofu: Soybean curd.

Tonyu: Soy milk.

Tosa-zu: Vinegar seasoned with dried bonito flakes.

Tosa-joyu: Tosa soy sauce, made by heating nikiri-zake with soy sauce and dried bonito flakes.

Tsukemono: Various kinds of salt-pickled vegetables such as cucumber, eggplants, Chinese cabbage, and daikon and so on.

Tsukune imo: A kind of yam.

Tsukushi: Horsetail stalks (*Equisetum arvense*) often eaten in spring in Japan as a dressed dish, simmered or in tempura.

U

Uguisuna: A kind of Kyoto greens (*Brassica campestris*)

Umami: The fifth flavor that humans can taste, said to be savory or meaty.

Ume: Sour Japanese apricots, usually called plums (*Prunus mume*) After harvesting, they are preserved with sugar or salt. Pickled with salt they are called *ume boshi*.

Uni: Sea urchin (*Euechinoidea*) its roe is eaten raw in sashimi or sushi. It can also be baked or steamed, and is considered a luxury item.

W

Wakame: seaweed. (*Undaria pinnatifida*) it is usually available salted or dried.

Warabi: Bracken fern shoots (*Pteridium aquilinum*) a wild plant that comes up in spring in Japan. The buds are eaten and starch produced from its rhizomes is used to make sweet dumplings.

Y

Yamaimo: Mountain potato (*Dioscorea japonica*) a long yam with a slimy texture.

Yuanji: A miso based marinade, aslo known as miso yuanji.

Yurine: Lily bulbs

Yuzu: A fragrant citrus hybrid (*Citrus junos/Citrus aurantium*) its skin is often used to add refreshing flavor and aroma.

Z

Zuiki: White taro stalks.

INDEX

Recipe page numbers in parentheses

ACKNOWLEDGMENTS

I am extremely grateful to many people for their kind support throughout the making of this book. First I would like to thank Kaoru Murakami, a bamboo shoot farmer. He is usually a very quiet person, but when it comes to bamboo shoots, he suddenly becomes a big talker. I think he just loves bamboo shoots.

I would like to thank Sayoko Eri, a living national treasure, who kindly gave me permission to use pictures of her *kirikane* works on the opening pages of each season. I also greatly appreciate the contribution of Kokei Eri.

It was my great pleasure to introduce a small part of Kyoto's rich culture through the photos of Kitano Tenmangu Shrine, Kodaiji Temple, Yasaka Jinja Shrine, and Ryuanji Temple, and I'd like to express my gratitude to those who gave us permission to photograph at those locations.

I sincerely thank two colleagues who took time to write forewords for the book, Ferran Adrià of elBulli and Chef Nobu Matsuhisa, who has popularized Japanese cuisine.

Many thanks to Masashi Kuma, the photographer who shot my dishes over the course of a year, and art director Kazuhiko Miki. Their patience, and the enthusiastic discussions that marked the shooting of each dish, were impressive.

A special thanks to Michiyuki Oba, the printing director who took great pains with the photos, and Hitomi Kato, who put my beliefs about and affection for cooking into a logical text. She always listened to my digressive stories with great patience.

I am also grateful for the support of Seigo Ito, and from Ritsumeikan University, Professor Yoshiyuki Ishibaji and Kazuko Hattori, a treasured customer at Kikunoi.

I also deeply appreciate the dauntless efforts of Shoko Imai and Steve Ford who worked on translating and editing, and Greg Starr, who oversaw the creation of my very first English cookbook. I give great thanks to the wonderful staff of Kodansha International.

Lastly, I must thank all the staff at Kikunoi.

Kikunoi (main restaurant)

Gion Maruyama Makuzugahara, Higashiyama-ku, Kyoto, Japan
Tel: 075–561–0015

Roan Kikunoi

Kiya-machi Shijo-sagaru, Shimogyo-ku, Kyoto, Japan
Tel: 075–361–5580

Akasaka Kikunoi

Akasaka 6–13–8, Minato-ku, Tokyo, Japan
Tel: 03–3568–6055

Gion Festival Photo p. 52 © KOICHIRO KITAOKU/A.collection/amana

(英文版)菊乃井 Kaiseki

2006年7月26日　第1刷発行

著　者　村田吉弘
撮　影　久間昌史
発行者　富田 充
発行所　講談社インターナショナル株式会社
〒112–8652 東京都文京区音羽 1–17–14
電話　03–3944–6493(編集部)
03–3944–6492(マーケティング部・業務部)
ホームページ　www.kodansha-intl.com

印刷・製本所　大日本印刷株式会社

Printed in Japan
ISBN 4–7700–3022–3